Advanced Vocabulary and Idiom

B J Thomas

Nelson

Thomas Nelson and Sons Ltd
Nelson House Mayfield Road
Walton-on-Thames Surrey
KT12 5PL UK

51 York Place
Edinburgh
EH1 3JD UK

Thomas Nelson (Hong Kong) Ltd
Toppan Building 10/F
22A Westlands Road
Quarry Bay Hong Kong

First published by Edward Arnold, a division of Hodder and
Stoughton Ltd 1989
Reprinted once. ISBN 0-340-50441-2

This edition first published by Thomas Nelson and Sons Ltd 1991

ISBN 0-17-556026-9
NPN 9 8 7 6 5 4

Printed in Great Britain by BPCC Wheatons Ltd, Exeter

Contents

Introduction

Topics

Related Word Groups

Word Formation

Problem Words

Idiom

Identification

Description

Style

Spoken English

Miscellaneous

INTRODUCTION

Advanced Vocabulary and Idiom is for students who already have a good command of the basic structures of English and who now wish to increase their range of vocabulary and idiom, and to gain more knowledge of particular styles of English. It gives invaluable assistance to students preparing for the Cambridge Certificate of Proficiency in English and other advanced examinations.

To the student

Advanced Vocabulary and Idiom presents words and phrases from a wide variety of topics and gives practice in different styles of English, such as formal, colloquial and slang, advertising and newspaper headlines. The types of exercises are varied and students are helped to understand not only what the words mean but also how they are used. Learners on their own should avoid going through the book mechanically. Exercises should be done at intervals and as a supplement to other materials and activities, and students should give themselves time to practise what they have learnt before going on to learn more. It is not satisfactory simply to complete the exercises and *understand* the new words in them. Learners must actually *use* the words in conversation, composition and letters before they can feel confident that these words are part of their active vocabulary.

To the teacher

Advanced Vocabulary and Idiom is divided into ten sections, each concentrating on a different aspect of vocabulary and its use. Word Formation contains exercises to increase awareness of how words are constructed. Problem Words is intended as a reference section to be used as and when problems arise with particular words or pairs of words. Related Word Groups introduces new words and phrases as useful preparation for conversation and composition on given subjects. Idiom introduces groups of common idiomatic words and phrases, and requires students to put them in the contexts provided. Identification contains brief comprehension exercises in particular areas of vocabulary. The Description exercises first provide practical comprehension practice based on certain kinds of common description, and then require students to use what they have learnt in this process by giving similar descriptions of their own. The exercises in Style assist students systematically to understand formal, colloquial and other more specialist forms of English and then, where it is useful, require them to produce the same kind of language themselves. Spoken English introduces certain common colloquial forms and will be especially useful for students who do not study in English-speaking countries and therefore do not have the advantage of hearing this kind of language around them. The Miscellaneous section contains a variety of exercises: Geo-political Names and Britain will help students to understand newspapers and other mass media; Names and Titles and Abbreviations give practical information about everyday English usage; Foreign Words and Phrases, Proverbs and Euphemisms provide useful knowledge of commonly-used expressions.

Advanced Vocabulary and Idiom can be used in a variety of ways. Time should be spent in class on a discussion of the subject matter of an exercise, the introduction and any examples it gives and the target words themselves. Only when the students understand what an exercise is about and have received any necessary help should they be required to attempt it themselves. The book is not best used as a series of mechanical tests. Exercises can be done as pair or group activities in class, leading to a discussion or other creative task. More straightforward exercises can be done as homework, with the aid of the key or a dictionary, in preparation for class discussion or work on a specific area of language.

TOPICS

City Life

Put each of the following words or phrases in its correct place in the passage below.

cosmopolitan	**pollution**	**congestion**	**to breed crime**
metropolis	**urban**	**cost of living**	**irresistible lure**
stimulation	**commuter**	**city-dwellers**	**anonymity**

Most people in developed countries are (a) _____, many drawn by the (b) _____ of the (c) _____. The attractions of the city are many: the (d) _____ atmosphere (foreign restaurants, different languages, international companies), the (e) _____ of cultural events or the simple hope of finding work. All too many find, however, that the glamorous façade is false. One can be very alone in the city and the (f) _____ which at first seems to give freedom and protection later leaves just loneliness. There is a lot to do but everything is expensive. The (g) _____ is high. There is (h) _____ not only of the physical but also of the moral environment and the various pressures of (i) _____ life cause cities (j) _____. Above all, perhaps, it is the daily stresses and strains of the city which make life there a matter of survival rather than of enjoyment. Many a (k) _____ struggling to work through the rush-hour (l) _____ asks, 'Is it worth it?'

Issues in Education

Put each of the following words or phrases in its correct place in the passage below.

elite	**divisive**	**potential**
gifted	**classless**	**spontaneity**
cram	**streaming**	**conventional**
labelled	**privileged**	**inferiority complex**

It is interesting that in some countries which are socialist and therefore supposedly (a) _____, the educational system is based on (b) _____, which means that children are educated according to their ability, with the more (c) _____ children separated from the others. Supporters of this system say that more intelligent children will be helped to achieve their full (d) _____ in this way and that these children will be held back if they have to share lessons with less clever pupils. Opponents of this system, on the other hand, maintain that it creates an educated (e) _____, a special class of (f) _____ people who are encouraged to think of themselves as superior to the others. Similarly the others may, as a result of being (g) _____ second-rate, develop some kind of (h) _____. In a word, such a system is (i) _____, since it creates a division between people. Another important question in education is the amount of freedom and choice children should be given at school. The conservative view is that a (j) _____ system of strict rules and fixed timetables is best. However, critics of this attitude say it causes regimentation, as in the army, and discourages children's natural imagination and (k) _____. We must ask ourselves what the purpose of education is: to (l) _____ children's heads with facts or to encourage them to develop their natural abilities in their own way?

Fashion in Clothes

Put each of the following words or phrases in its correct place in the passage below.

slavishly	trends	slaves to fashion
individualists	trendy	fashion houses
conformists	dictate	the latest fashion
haute couture	dictates	personal ornaments

Most people like to think they are (a) _____ and simply wear whatever they like. Few people will admit to being (b) _____. However we are not just talking of the expensive (c) _____ of the Paris and Milan (d) _____, which not many people can afford anyway. We are talking of fashions and (e) _____ in everyday clothes. We say that we wear jeans and sweaters because they are cheap and practical, but isn't it true that our jeans and sweaters tend to be the same as everyone else wears? Doesn't that mean that we like to be (f) _____? Of course the big chain-stores, to some extent, (g) _____ what we wear, but they always offer a choice and people do, on the whole, like to wear (h) _____, which extends beyond clothes to make-up, (i) _____ (men wear earrings too, nowadays) and hair-styles. It is easy to declare that we do not (j) _____ follow the (k) _____ of fashion, but aren't we all (l) _____ at heart?

Compulsory Military Service

Put each of the following words or phrases in its correct place in the passage below.

volunteers	pacifist	controversial	disruption
conscripts	discipline	voluntary	conscientious
professional	initiative	conscription	objector
amateur			

(a) _____, which simply means compulsory military service, is a very (b) _____ issue. People constantly argue for and against it. Its supporters say that it gives young men a sense of (c) _____ in a world where the young increasingly have too much freedom. They say it helps young men, who perhaps were tied to their mothers' apron-strings at home, to stand on their own feet and encourages them to develop (d) _____, since a young soldier must make his own decisions and cannot rely on his parents to tell him what to do. Opponents of compulsory military service argue that an army of (e) _____ is an unsatisfactory, (f) _____ one, since one cannot expect reluctant young men to perform war-time duties efficiently after only a year or two of training. A war, they say, must be fought by a (g) _____ army, and soldiers should all be (h) _____. Compulsory military service for all young men also causes (i) _____ to the education and careers of the young, since it creates a gap just when they should be studying or starting work. Finally there is the problem of the young man who is against war on principle. In other words he is a (j) _____. In Britain a person who refuses to do military service is called a (k) _____. If his reasons are accepted, he may be obliged to perform other, non-military duties but it is a difficult position for anyone to be in and it does not come about if military service is (l) _____.

Advertising

Put each of the following words or phrases in its correct place below.

beneficial   misleading   blatant   brainwash
implicit   catchy jingles   exploit   ubiquitous
bombard   watch-dog   subtle   informative

Modern advertisements contain hidden messages. (a) _____ in the advertisement showing the pretty girl in the new car or the smiling children round the packet of washing powder is the message that if we buy the product, we also achieve success and happiness. It is a (b) _____ approach since it seeks to (c) _____ our secret dreams, and it is inescapable since advertising is (d) _____. Giant street hoardings and (e) _____ on television (f) _____ us from all sides. They (g) _____ us into believing that we can realize our ambitions quickly and easily. On the other hand, defenders of advertising say that it is (h) _____. Advertising is (i) _____. Advertisements tell us about useful new products. They brighten our lives with colour and music. They increase demand, stimulate industry and so keep prices down. Whether for or against advertising, most people would agree that some kind of (j) _____ body, appointed by the government or by the advertising industry itself, is necessary to maintain standards of honesty and to discourage the more (k) _____ types of (l) _____ advertisements.

How Much Freedom Should Children Have?

Put each of the following words or phrases in its correct place below.

possessive   upbringing   permissive   rebelliousness
suppress   formative   juvenile   run wild
inhibited   authoritarian   delinquency   adolescence

It is often said that we live in a (a) _____ age, one in which people are allowed to do almost anything they like. Is this good for children? They are going through their (b) _____, which is a very (c) _____ stage of their development since their final adult characters are beginning to take shape. Some parents think it is good for children to be allowed to (d) _____, without control or supervision. They say that this enables children's personalities to develop naturally and that they will learn to be responsible by the mistakes they make. However, this might lead to (e) _____, with the children ending up in the courts, or it might simply make children self-centred, without any consideration for others. Other parents believe in being strict, but taken to extremes this can produce a too (f) _____ atmosphere in the home, with the children being dominated and ruled by their parents. Parents can also be very (g) _____ and try to keep their children dependent on them. These last two attitudes can encourage (h) _____ (against parents, school, authority) in a child, or, conversely, (i) _____ a child's natural sense of adventure and curiosity. A strict (j) _____ by over-caring parents can make a child so timid and (k) _____ that he or she is unable to express freely his or her emotions and form mature relationships. To bring up children to be normal, well-adjusted human beings requires great wisdom, and perhaps a bit of luck.

Censorship

Put each of the following words or phrases in its correct place below.

perverted   **moral**   **banned**   **masquerading**
excessive   **standards**   **degrades**   **unscrupulous**
counter-   **infringes**   **corrupting**   **gratuitous**
 productive   **safeguards**

The amount of offensive material we are exposed to in films nowadays is surely (a) _____. Most people accept that scenes of sex and violence are sometimes necessary to tell a story, but all too often these scenes are (b) _____; they are unnecessary and simply inserted in the film to appeal to the baser human instincts. Censorship is necessary, especially to protect children from the (c) _____ influence of such scenes, often (d) _____ as art, in our cinemas. There should also be censorship of pornographic magazines produced by (e) _____ people willing to cater to the (f) _____ tastes of a small minority. Such material destroys the innocence of the young and (g) _____ all who read it. On the other hand, there are those who say that something which is (h) _____ becomes desirable so censorship is (i) _____, and that censorship (j) _____ on our freedom of choice. However freedom is not merely freedom to do what we want but freedom from attempts to destroy society's (k) _____. Censorship provides the (l) _____ by which society protects itself.

Love

Put each of the following words in its correct place below.

partners   **platonic**   **flirtation**   **infatuation**
mature   **compatible**   **one-sided**   **hero-worship**
mutual   **idolize**   **complement**   **stable**

Youngsters in their teens or even earlier sometimes (a) _____ film stars or other celebrities with a kind of blind, devoted (b) _____. The objects of such adoration are regarded as gods by their smitten worshippers. How sad that such devotion is almost always unrequited (though pop-stars have been known to marry their fans). Young people also sometimes develop an irrational obsession for another, often older, person which is not an adult, (c) _____ feeling but simply a youthful (d) _____. At parties a boy may playfully try to attract a girl, or vice versa, without intending any serious, lasting relationship. This is just a (e) _____. A relationship which gives deep and lasting happiness to both (f) _____ must not be (g) _____ (felt more strongly by one of the pair than by the other). It should be based on a (h) _____ love and respect, felt equally by each of the two. Of course it can take many forms. It might be very deep but entail no physical desire, in which case it is described as (i) _____. Certainly, for any relationship to be (j) _____, the two people involved must be k) _____ (they must get on well together). This does not necessarily mean that they must have attitudes and interests in common, for partnerships of opposites can work very well. The different characters of the two people somehow (l) _____ each other.

Attitudes to Work and Leisure

Put each of the following words or phrases in its correct place below.

constructively	rewarding	challenge	conditioned
aimless	initiative	creativity	9 to 5
regimentation	scope	aspire	fulfilment

Most adults (a) _____ to more leisure but, in fact, not many people have the necessary (b) _____ to use the free time they already have very (c) _____. The sad fact is that we need work because it imposes the discipline we need. Life seems (d) _____ and we secretly look forward to our work again. We dream about personal (e) _____ but probably find it more in our work than in our leisure time. This depends on age. The young are free from work and responsibility, and freedom comes naturally to them. However, after they begin jobs they become (f) _____ to work. They find they need it, however much they complain about its routine and (g) _____. Obviously this again depends on the kind of work. Those with (h) _____ jobs, or jobs which require (i) _____, receive genuine satisfaction from their work, but most of us are in conventional (j) _____ jobs which offer little (k) _____ for imagination. We leave our work only to face a leisure that we find difficult to cope with. Our mistake is in regarding leisure as a chance to do nothing, whereas in fact it should be looked on as a (l) _____.

The Purpose of State Punishment

Put each of the following words or phrases in its correct place below.

wrongdoer	deterrent	law-abiding	death penalty
misdeeds	reform	crime doesn't	corporal
barbaric	retribution	pay	punishment
humane	rehabilitate		

What is the purpose of punishment? One purpose is obviously to (a) _____ the offender, to correct the offender's moral attitudes and anti-social behaviour and to (b) _____ him or her, which means to assist the offender to return to normal life as a useful member of the community. Punishment can also be seen as a (c) _____, because it warns other people of what will happen if they are tempted to break the law and so prevents them from doing so. However, a third purpose of punishment lies, perhaps, in society's desire for (d) _____, which basically means revenge. In other words, don't we feel that a (e) _____ should suffer for his (f) _____? The form of punishment should also be considered. On the one hand, some believe that we should 'make the punishment fit the crime'. Those who steal from others should be deprived of their own property to ensure that criminals are left in no doubt that (g) '_____'. For those who attack others, (h) _____ should be used. Murderers should be subject to the principle 'an eye for an eye and a tooth for a tooth' and automatically receive the (i) _____. On the other hand, it is said that such views are unreasonable, cruel and (j) _____ and that we should show a more (k) _____ attitude to punishment and try to understand why a person commits a crime and how society has failed to enable him to live a respectable, (l) _____ life.

Women's Rights

Put each of the following words or phrases in its correct place in the passage below.

male chauvinist	male-dominated	unisex	exploitation
second-class citizens	the weaker sex	feminist	discrimination
	militant	sexist	battle of the sexes
		sex-objects	

A (a) _____ is a person, usually a woman, who believes that women should be regarded as equal to men. She, or he, deplores (b) _____ against women in the home, place of work or anywhere, and her principal enemy is the (c) _____, who believes that men are naturally superior. Tired of being referred to as (d) '_____', women are becoming more and more (e) _____ and are winning the age-old (f) _____. They are sick to death of (g) _____ jokes which poke fun at women. They are no longer content to be regarded as (h) _____ in terms of economic, political and social status. They criticize beauty-contests and the use of glamorous female models in advertisements, which they describe as the (i) _____ of female beauty, since women in these situations are represented as mere (j) _____. We no longer live in the (k) _____ societies of the past. Let us hope, however, that the revolution stops before we have a boring world in which sex doesn't make much difference. We already have (l) _____ hairdressers and fashions. What next?

Modern Values

Put each of the following words or phrases in its correct place in the passage below.

status	image	welfare state	mercenary
affluence	acquisitive	motivated	spiritual
priorities	materialistic	idealism	status-symbols

People nowadays have more money, and some say this new (a) _____ has made people more (b) _____, which means they place too much importance on money, comfort and luxury goods, and more (c) _____, which means they want to buy, own, possess more and more. We are not only money-oriented but also over-concerned with social and professional (d) _____. We care too much about our (e) _____, how other people see us. We like to own (f) _____ like unnecessarily fast cars, the latest hi-fi equipment, fashionable clothes. Another factor is that many of us now live in a (g) _____, in which all our basic needs are provided by the government. In fact, care for those in need is now so highly organized that there is less scope for personal (h) _____. What can a mere individual do to improve the world? But is the picture so black? Are we really reduced to being (i) _____ creatures, (j) _____ only by money? Perhaps it is time we examined our (k) _____ and decided what is really important in life. Perhaps we should try to find self-fulfilment by exploring our capabilities and finding satisfaction in the (l) _____ aspects of life: an appreciation of art and nature, service to others, the improvement of our minds.

RELATED WORD GROUPS

Body

Divide the following 24 words into three equal groups under the headings a) head b) arm and hand c) leg and foot.

jaw	lash	pupil	lobe
elbow	shin	temple	knuckles
calf	forearm	wrist	toes
thigh	thumb	heel	gums
biceps	instep	fist	ankle
lid	palm	sole	nostril

Books

Types of Book **1** Put each of the following words in its correct place below.

volume	publication	whodunnit	hardback
best-seller	thriller	copy	edition
manuscript	proofs	paperback	

(a) You can see the original _____ of *Hamlet* in the museum in Shakespeare's own writing.

(b) Before a book is sent to be printed, the author must check the _____.

(c) Where is _____ three of this set of encyclopaedias?

(d) The new government report on agricultural statistics is a very interesting _____.

(e) Have you got a _____ of Graham Greene's *Brighton Rock*?

(f) This book costs £12, but that's the _____ price. The _____ costs only £5.50.

(g) His first three novels didn't sell very well, but his fourth was a _____ and made a fortune.

(h) The book has already been selling well for five years. Now the publishers are going to bring out a new _____ with illustrations.

(i) She likes to relax by reading a _____ about spies or crime.

(j) I'm reading a _____. It's fun trying to guess who the murderer is.

2 Answer the following questions using the words at the top of the exercise above.

E.g. What might a publisher do if one of his books is chosen as a school or exam test?
He might bring out a special *edition* with notes and test questions.

(a) Why is an encyclopaedia usually more expensive than a dictionary?

(b) What is a murder mystery called, and why?

(c) What is an exciting adventure story called, and why?

(d) How can you get information about scientific, technical, statistical and similar matters?

(e) How would you ask for a particular book in a bookshop?

(f) What must an author do when a publisher's deadline arrives?

(g) What must be done before a book is printed?

(h) What does every author hope?

(i) How can you save money when buying books?

Ways of reading 3 Put each of the following words or phrases into its correct place in the sentences below.

skip	look up	browse	read from
skim	dip into	wade through	cover to
flip through	refer to	peruse	cover

(a) I spend a lot of time in bookshops. I don't often buy books. I just _____.

(b) If I come to a boring bit in a book, I just _____ a few pages till the real story starts again.

(c) I'll _____ his number in the phone-book.

(d) I didn't know the word. I had to _____ a dictionary.

(e) Of course an encyclopaedia is not a book you _____. You just _____ it for things that interest you.

(f) I never liked history at school. I found it very hard to _____ all that boring stuff about wars and revolutions.

(g) We have requested our lawyers to _____ the document with the greatest care to decide whether it's legal or not.

(h) Some people have the ability to _____ a page, which means to read it very quickly, just taking in the main points.

(i) I sometimes _____ a magazine in a newsagent's but I don't usually buy one.

4 Using one or more items from the list at the top of the exercise above, explain how you use each of the following.

E.g. a novel
If it's good, I *read it from cover to cover*, but sometimes I *skip* long, descriptive passages.

(a) a dictionary
(b) a magazine
(c) an encyclopaedia
(d) a contract
(e) an atlas
(f) a guidebook
(g) a photograph album
(h) a newspaper
(i) a car maintenance manual

5 Answer the questions below from the following list of parts of a book.

acknowledge- ments	'blurb'	key	glossary
appendix	contents	footnotes	chronology
bibliography	dedication	frontispiece	index

In what part of a book would you look to find . . .

(a) . . . answers to exercise questions?
(b) . . . who supplied the photographs or helped with special research?
(c) . . . quickly what the book is about?
(d) . . . meanings of foreign or technical expressions used in the text?
(e) . . . on what page a person, place or event is mentioned?
(f) . . . if the book was written for a particular person?
(g) . . . extra information about something mentioned in the main text?
(h) . . . what other books have been written on the same subject?
(i) . . . a picture of the author or the subject of the book?
(j) . . . how the book is organized in chapters?
(k) . . . a convenient list of the dates and events of the period covered in the book?

Dirt and Damage

1 Put each of the following adjectives in its correct place in the sentences below.

blunt	**scratched**	**smeared**	**shabby**
torn	**shop-soiled**	**filthy**	**soiled**
rusty	**stained**	**smudged**	**faded**

(a) He was very angry when he saw that his new car was _____.
Another car must have run along the side of it.

(b) The curtains were bright red when we bought them, but they've
become _____ in the strong sunlight.

(c) That jacket needs cleaning and it's rather old. I think it's too _____
to wear.

(d) If you have a banknote which is _____ in two, take it to a bank and
exchange it for a new one.

(e) Buy our new design 'Travelbag'. The different compartments will
enable the traveller to keep clean and _____ garments separate.

(f) When she was two years old, she used to experiment with her
mother's lipstick. Her face was always _____ with it.

(g) See those red-brown bits? That's where the machine is beginning
to go _____ because it's unprotected from the rain.

(h) You can see the ceiling is _____ where the rain came through.

(i) This radio is a bit _____ after being in the shop for nine months, so
I'll knock 10% off the price.

(j) Let the ink dry before you put another piece of paper on top of it.
Otherwise it'll be _____.

(k) This knife isn't sharp, it's _____. Give me another one.

(l) This shirt isn't just dirty, Bobby. It's absolutely _____!

2 Using words from the list at the top of the exercise above, say what
kind of damage or wear the following items can suffer.

(a) a photograph
(b) a book
(c) a car in an accident
(d) a car after long use
(e) a coat
(f) a television set
(g) a piece of furniture
(h) a razor-blade

Drinking

1 Make sentences by connecting each person on the left below with the correct phrase on the right.

(a) A teetotaller	serves people in a pub.
(b) A secret drinker	runs a pub.
(c) A social drinker	has a drink from time to time.
(d) An occasional drinker	only drinks with other people, e.g. at parties.
(e) An alcoholic	doesn't want other people to know he drinks.
(f) A drunkard	drinks a lot.
(g) A 'wino'	is often drunk.
(h) A heavy drinker	never drinks alcohol.
(i) A publican	produces beer in large quantities.
(j) A barmaid	is addicted to alcohol.
(k) A brewer	is a poor person, often homeless, who drinks anything, anywhere.

2 The dangers of alcoholism are very real. Put the people in the above exercise (on the left) in order of the danger they are in from alcoholism, with those in greatest danger at the top. Then draw a line between those you think are safe from alcoholism and those who might become, or already are, in danger from this disease.

3 Match each drink on the left below with its description on the right.

(a) squash	a last (alcoholic) drink before going to bed
(b) a cocktail	a non-alcoholic fruit drink
(c) a nightcap	a mixture of beer and lemonade (or a similar drink)
(d) one for the road	a mixture of wine or spirits and hot water, sugar, lemon etc.
(e) a shandy	a refreshing non-alcoholic drink, e.g. squash, Coca-Cola
(f) punch	a single drink of spirits
(g) a soft drink	a mixed alcoholic drink
(h) a short	a last drink before driving

4 From the list of drinks on the left above, choose one or more which would be a good drink for. . .

(a) . . . a children's party.
(b) . . . an adults' party.
(c) . . . a formal reception.
(d) . . . someone who's going to drive.
(e) . . . a last drink of the evening.
(f) . . . a hot day.
(g) . . . someone who is nervous before an important occasion.
(h) . . . someone who is trying to give up alcohol.

5 Put each of the following words into its correct place in the sentences below.

sip	**pub crawl**	**toast**	**breathalyzer**
drop	**stagger**	**booze**	**corkscrew**
intoxicated	**vineyard**	**cheers**	**hangover**

(a) Let's open another bottle of wine. Where's the _____?
(b) We went on a _____ last night. This morning I've got a terrible _____.
(c) Wine is made from grapes, which are grown in a _____.
(d) Here's a _____ to John and Elizabeth.
(e) Don't drink it all at once. Just _____ it.
(f) When British people drink, they often say, '_____'.
(g) The police stopped the driver and gave him a _____ test.
(h) I don't want much, please, just a _____.
(i) A slang word for alcoholic drink is '_____'.
(j) A formal word for 'drunk' is '_____'.
(k) He couldn't walk properly. He could only _____.

6 Briefly describe, as a warning of the possible dangers of alcohol, an evening in which some people start drinking and end up in a police cell. Use at least six of the words at the top of the exercise above.

7 Explain the difference in each of the following pairs.

(a) sober and drunk
(b) tipsy and drunk
(c) still orange and fizzy orange
(d) draught beer and bottled beer
(e) 'on the wagon' and teetotal
(f) vintage wine and 'plonk'
(g) a pub and an off-licence
(h) neat whisky and whisky 'on the rocks'
(i) 'Dutch courage' and 'to go Dutch'

Driving

1 Put each of the following verbs, in the past tense, in its correct place in the passage below.

accelerate	fasten	pull up	sound
adjust	dip	release	skid
apply	indicate	reverse	start up
check	overtake	swerve	turn on

Another hundred miles to go. Dark night. Heavy traffic. He glanced at the dashboard. He was OK for fuel and well within the speed-limit. He (a) _____ that he was pulling out, put his foot down, (b) _____ and (c) _____ two cars in front. It began to rain. He (d) _____ the wind-screen wipers and settled back comfortably into the leather upholstery. For a moment he was mesmerized by the rhythmic movement of the wipers. He looked at the road ahead. An oncoming car! He (e) _____ his head-lights but was dazzled by the other driver's. He (f) _____ his horn. The other car seemed to be coming straight towards him! He (g) _____ to avoid it. He was confused. He (h) _____ his brakes, but (i) _____ on the wet surface. He went off the road and collided with a tree. Slowly he (j) _____ onto the road again, drove ten metres forward and (k) _____. He got out and inspected the car for damage. Some scratches on the bodywork. Dented bumper. He lifted the bonnet and (l) _____ the engine. It appeared to be OK. He got into the car again, (m) _____ his seat-belt, (n) _____ the mirror and (o) _____ the engine nervously. It purred sweetly. Good. He (p) _____ the hand-brake. The car moved forward. Another hundred miles to go.

2 Describe how you failed your driving test disastrously.

Food

Ways of Eating　**1** Put each of the following verbs into its correct place in the sentences below.

chew	lick	polish off	swallow
gnaw	consume	peck at	gorge
digest	bolt		

(a) The children have no appetite. They just _____ their food. They hardly eat anything.
(b) My mother always used to say to me, 'Now make sure you _____ meat carefully before you _____ it.'
(c) In Britain people _____ four million tons of potatoes every year.
(d) He has an enormous appetite. I've seen him _____ four hamburgers and a pile of chips at a sitting.
(e) As children we used to _____ ourselves on ice-cream, chips and chocolate, and then feel very sick.
(f) The starving prisoners were so desperate they would _____ any meat bones they could find.
(g) It's not good for your body to _____ your food so quickly. Eat slowly so that you can _____ it properly.

(h) He was so hungry that when he'd finished his food, he began to
_____ the plate!

2   Answer the following questions using words from the list at the top of
exercise 1.

(a) How do people eat ice-cream cones?
(b) How do hungry people eat?
(c) How do very greedy people eat?
(d) How do people eat if they are not very hungry?
(e) How do dogs eat?
(f) What is a good, healthy way to eat meat?
(g) What is an unhealthy way to eat, and why?

Meats

3   Some meat is given a different name from the animal it comes from.
What animals do the following meats come from?

(a) pork
(b) beef
(c) bacon
(d) venison

(e) veal
(f) mutton
(g) ham

**Food
preparation**

4   Match each verb on the left below with the food item on the right it is
most often associated with.

(a) to pluck	cheese
(b) to crack	an orange
(c) to grate	a chicken
(d) to knead	a nut
(e) to peel	a rabbit
(f) to skin	a joint of meat
(g) to slice	dough
(h) to carve	a loaf

5   Instructions as above.

(a) to mince	cream
(b) to shell	meat
(c) to toss	a hard-boiled egg
(d) to whip	eggs
(e) to stuff	a cake
(f) to mash	a chicken
(g) to beat	a pancake
(h) to ice	potatoes

6   Explain the difference between the words or phrases in each of the
following pairs.

(a) starving and parched
(b) a snack and a square meal
(c) stale and mouldy
(d) peckish and ravenous
(e) uneatable and inedible
(f) a beer-bottle and a bottle of beer
(g) a starter and a dessert
(h) a restaurant and a café

Friends

1   The following is a list of different kinds of friends (and a few associates and enemies). Put each one in the most suitable space in the sentences below. Some words must be used more than once.

acquaintance	foe	associate	old flame
compatriot	partner	bosom pal	fair-weather
confidant	mate	pen-pal	friend
colleague	rival	companion	

(a) She comes from the same country as me. She's a _____.
(b) We carried on a friendship through letters. He was a _____.
(c) I'd rather not make the journey alone. I need a travelling- _____.
(d) He and I own this business together. He's my _____.
(e) She didn't know what the homework was so she asked a class-
      _____.
(f)   I've known George for ages. We're really good old friends who spend a lot of time together. He's my _____.
(g) Henry Somers wants the manager's job and so do I. He's my _____.
(h) Wanted: sensible, well-mannered girl to act as old lady's _____.
(i)   She used to be John's girl-friend. She's an _____.
(j)   The assistant to a plumber, electrician or lorry driver is known as his _____.
(k) In the darkness the soldier couldn't see whether the approaching figure was friend or _____.
(l)   She teaches in the same school as I do. She's a _____.
(m) He seems a good friend when things are going well, but when I'm in trouble he's nowhere to be seen. I'm afraid he's a _____.
(n) He's the person to whom I tell my most personal thoughts, problems and fears. He's my _____.
(o) If you can't afford to live on your own, you'll have to find a flat-
      _____.
(p) I don't really know him very well. He's just an _____.
(q) I just meet him occasionally when his firm and my firm work together. He's just a business _____.

2   Which people from the list at the top of the exercise above would you . . .

(a) . . . talk business with?
(b) . . . go to with personal problems?
(c) . . . visit on holiday?
(d) . . . go on holiday with?
(e) . . . not trust?
(f)   . . . borrow money from?
(g) . . . invite to your party?
(h) . . . invite to your wedding?

Light

1 Put each word in its correct space in the sentences below.

flicker	twinkle	flash	sparkle
spark	floodlight	glow	flare
dazzle	lightning		

(a) The town council has decided to _____ the castle in summer for the benefit of tourists.
(b) Stand back when I put petrol on the fire. It will make it _____ up.
(c) I saw the _____ of a lighted cigarette in the darkness.
(d) He was killed by a _____ of _____ during a thunderstorm.
(e) The stars do not give off a constant light. They seem to _____.
(f) Put on dark glasses or the sun will _____ you and you won't be able to see.
(g) The candle flame began to _____ a little in the wind.
(h) In very dry weather just a small _____ from a passing train can start a forest fire.
(i) Look how the jewels in her crown _____ as she moves.

2 Instructions as above.

spotlight	chandelier	traffic-lights	searchlight
limelight	torch	son et lumière	headlights
footlights	lantern		

(a) It was too dark to drive safely without the _____ on.
(b) The bus stopped at the _____.
(c) The usherette showed us to our seats in the cinema with her _____.
(d) Every summer they have a _____ show at the Tower of London for tourists.
(e) Famous people spend their lives in the _____.
(f) The _____ in a theatre are along the front of the stage.
(g) She was illuminated in the middle of the dark stage by a single _____.
(h) The anti-aircraft unit used a powerful _____ to light up the sky and show any enemy planes.
(i) The large room was very grand. It was lit by an enormous _____ containing about 200 lights.
(j) 200 years ago, if you went out at night you carried a _____, which was a candle or oil-light inside a metal and glass container.

Materials

1 Match each material on the left below with the most appropriate word, phrase or phrases on the right.

(a) corduroy	a ship's sail, a boxing ring
(b) canvas	church windows
(c) denim	the roof of a shed or cheap hut
(d) fur	comfortable soft trousers
(e) frosted glass	jeans
(f) stained glass	bathroom windows
(g) corrugated iron	a woman's expensive, warm coat
(h) straw	cutlery
(i) brick	a man's old-fashioned light summer hat
(j) stainless steel	a wall

2 Instructions as above.

(a) cork	old ships
(b) silk	packing material
(c) suede	fine cups, saucers, dishes
(d) linen	a wine-bottle stopper
(e) serge	shoes, a casual jacket
(f) corrugated cardboard	a lawn
(g) tweed	a woman's expensive evening dress
(h) porcelain	fine bed-sheets
(i) timber	a man's hard-wearing sports-jacket
(j) turf	an ordinary soldier's uniform

3 What materials, from those in the exercises above, might the following items be made of?

(a) a football pitch
(b) a man's tie
(c) table-mats
(d) the lining of a winter coat
(e) a woman's casual skirt
(f) tents
(g) a household lamp base
(h) a dentist's surgery windows
(i) a watch-case
(j) a table-cloth
(k) an overcoat
(l) a house
(m) an oil-painting base
(n) a woman's purse
(o) a cheap casual jacket
(p) a baby's toy animal

Memory

1 Put each of the following words or phrases in its correct place in the sentences below.

reminisce	sieve	total recall	memorable
absent-minded	haunt	nostalgia	lasting
cast	blank		

(a) The terrible things he saw in the war still _____ him.
(b) Old people often feel a strong _____ for the days of their youth.
(c) The words of his old teacher left a _____ impression in his mind. He is still influenced by them.
(d) We often sit around and _____ about the old days when we were young.
(e) If you will _____ your minds back to 1982, you will remember that. . .
(f) His memory was amazing. He forgot nothing. He seemed to have _____.
(g) I'm afraid I can't remember. I've got a memory like a _____.
(h) I'll never forget that day. It was a very _____ occasion.
(i) When I looked at the exam-paper, I couldn't remember a thing. My mind was a complete _____.
(j) He sometimes puts salt in his tea instead of sugar. He's very _____.

2 What do the following phrases mean?

(a) It's on the tip of my tongue.
(b) I racked my brains.
(c) Does this name ring a bell?
(d) I clean forgot the appointment.
(e) She has a photographic memory.
(f) I know the poem by heart.

Money

Coins, notes and banks

1 Put each of the following words or phrases in its correct place in the sentences below.

numismatist	standing order	currency	expenditure
counterfoil	counterfeit	statement	bounce
legal tender			

(a) You can change your _____ at any bank or large hotel.
(b) She held the note up to the light to make sure it wasn't _____.
(c) He collects coins and banknotes. He's a _____.
(d) I always fill in the _____ when I write out a cheque. Otherwise I would lose track of my _____.
(e) I don't trust him. I'm sure his cheque will _____.
(f) I pay my rent by _____. It saves me having to write a cheque every month.
(g) The bank sends me a detailed _____ every month.
(h) Don't worry. Scottish banknotes are _____ in England too.

2 Instructions as above.

| broke | quid | hire purchase | make ends meet |
| chickenfeed | I.O.U. | mortgage | instalments |

(a) I'm afraid I have no money at all. I'm completely _____.

(b) She finds London very expensive. She says she can't _____ on less than £100 a week.

(c) To a multi-millionaire £100 is _____.

(d) Can you lend me a couple of _____?

(e) I managed to get a _____ to buy a house. I'll be paying it back for the next 20 years.

(f) He lent me the money but he didn't trust me completely and asked me to give him an _____.

(g) I couldn't really afford to buy a car so I got it on _____ and paid monthly _____ until it was finally mine.

3 Use at least five of the words at the top of the above exercise and any you like from Exercise 1 to describe, in a short paragraph, someone's terrible financial situation.

Numbers

Put each of the following words in its correct place in the sentences below.

digits	round	even	ordinal
scores	Roman	good	cardinal
odd	dozen	average	hat-trick
odd	gross		

(a) He's a very good footballer. He scored a _____ in the last game and nearly got a fourth goal.

(b) It was after midnight but there were still _____ of people in the streets.

(c) 1,2,3,4,5 etc. are _____ numbers. 1st, 2nd, 3rd, 4th, 5th etc. are _____ numbers.

(d) Could you go and buy a _____ eggs, please?

(e) Each packet contains a _____ of paper-clips.

(f) I, II, III, IV etc. are known as _____ numerals.

(g) 2, 4, 6, 8, 10 etc. are _____ numbers. 1, 3, 5, 7, 9 etc. are _____ numbers.

(h) There are normally seven _____ in a London telephone number.

(i) There were twenty- _____ people at the meeting. I don't know exactly how many.

(j) It was a bargain. I paid £10 but it was worth a _____ fifteen.

(k) The students' ages vary. The _____ is about 22.

(l) OK, I'll lend you the £95 you need. Well, let's make it a _____ number. Here's £100.

People

1 Match each of the following colloquial names for certain types of people with the correct description below.

a pain in the neck	a crank	a lone wolf	a dare-devil
a rolling stone	a busybody	a sponger	a battle-axe
a slow coach	a tomboy	a day-dreamer	a golden boy

(a) He's always got his head in the clouds, always fantasizing.
(b) She's very inquisitive about my private life.
(c) He loves taking dangerous risks.
(d) He can't settle down. He goes from job to job, place to place.
(e) He's always borrowing money and living off other people.
(f) She's very aggressive and bossy. She likes to dominate.
(g) Everyone thinks he'll get rapid promotion. He's destined to succeed.
(h) He's always slow and behind the others in his work or studies.
(i) She's got extremely odd, eccentric, unconventional ideas and theories.
(j) He's a real nuisance. I can't stand him.
(k) He likes to do things on his own.
(l) She's a girl who likes to play rough, boys' games.

2 Instructions as above.

a tear-away	a clock-watcher	a layabout	a miser
a wind-bag	a name-dropper	a litter-lout	a slave-driver
a slob		a road-hog	
a jay-walker		a fare-dodger	

(a) She talks on and on about her opinions and ideas.
(b) He keeps count of every penny he has and only spends money if he must.
(c) She likes to mention all the famous and important people she's met.
(d) He makes his employees work extremely hard.
(e) She crosses the road without bothering to look at the traffic.
(f) He's lazy and prefers not to work.
(g) She drops rubbish anywhere and never puts it in the bin.
(h) He drives very inconsiderately of other drivers.
(i) She's only interested in leaving work and going home.
(j) She avoids paying when she travels on public transport.
(k) He dresses and behaves in a very careless, often disgusting, way.
(l) He's a bit wild, always getting into fights and other trouble.

Small Quantities

1 The following words represent small pieces or quantities. Put each in its correct place in the sentences below. Some words must be used more than once.

glimmer	**grain**	**fragment**	**dot**
shred	**crumb**	**blade**	**trace**
speck			

(a) She was very houseproud. There wasn't a _____ of dirt in her kitchen.

(b) They were so hungry they ate the whole loaf of bread without letting a single _____ fall to the ground.

(c) The desert stretched for miles. Nothing green. Not a single _____ of grass.

(d) We watched the ship as it sailed away until it was just a _____ on the horizon.

(e) His views are dangerous and extreme, and yet there is a _____ of truth in what he says.

(f) The accusations against him are completely groundless. There isn't a _____ of evidence to support them.

(g) Archeologists are examining a _____ of a vase which they think is over 5,000 years old.

(h) There now seems to be a _____ of hope that the strike will be averted.

(i) The famine is so bad in that area that the people haven't seen a single _____ of rice for weeks.

(j) One day in June 1987, he suddenly disappeared without _____ and no one has seen him since.

(k) The police found a tiny _____ of lipstick on the wineglass.

2 Instructions as above.

hint	**clue**	**breath**	**flake**
drop	**puff**	**dash**	**item**
scrap			

(a) 'Whisky?' 'Well, just a _____, please.'

(b) Don't ask me about the economic situation. I haven't a _____.

(c) I'm just going out for a _____ of fresh air.

(d) I watched a rain- _____ trickling slowly down the window.

(e) I'd like my coffee almost black, please. Just a very small _____ of milk.

(f) 'What a lovely smell. What is it?' 'Some spices and I think some seafood and also just a _____ of lemon.'

(g) I wrote the phone-number down on a _____ of paper I tore from an envelope.

(h) Everything was very still. Not a leaf moved. There wasn't the smallest _____ of wind.

(i) After a meal they always gave any _____s of left-over food to the dog.

(j) Here's an interesting _____ of news about a boy who found £500 in the street.

(k) If you put a snow- _____ under a special microscope, you will see it has a wonderful pattern.

Social Types

1 The following is a list of colloquial names for various social types, i.e. different kinds of people one meets at parties and elsewhere. Use the most suitable one to complete each description below.

wet blanket	**Don Juan**	**gate-crasher**	**life and soul of**
wallflower	**chatterbox**	**good mixer**	**the party**
social climber	**femme fatale**	**gossip**	

(a) He's very lively and the centre of any group he's in. People always have a good time when he's there. He's the _____.

(b) She's so negative and boring. She has a depressing effect on any group of people she's with. She's a _____.

(c) She's confident and interested in other people. She likes to meet different kinds of people. She's a _____.

(d) He goes to parties and other occasions without an invitation. He just walks in. He's a _____.

(e) Unfortunately she is not usually asked to dance by anyone. She just stands there hoping. She's a _____.

(f) He just can't stop talking. He goes on and on excitedly, about totally unimportant things. He's a _____.

(g) He loves to discuss and pass on news or rumours about people's private lives. He's a _____.

(h) She's dangerously attractive to men. Half the men she meets fall in love with her. She's a _____.

(i) He knows he's attractive to women. They always fall for him. He's got lots of girl-friends. He's a _____.

(j) She's very conscious of her social position and is always trying to improve it by meeting 'upper-class' people. She's a _____.

2 What type or types of person from the list at the top of the exercise above . . .

(a) . . . would be good to have at a party?

(b) . . . would you especially avoid?

(c) . . . might have a lot of romantic relationships?

(d) . . . makes friends easily?

(e) . . . would get on well together? (make pairs, e.g. Don Juan and femme fatale)

(f) . . . are you?

3 Instructions as in Exercise 1.

parasite	**good company**	**bore**	**early bird**
socialite	**loner**	**killjoy**	**jet-setter**
trouble-maker	**snob**		

(a) He's a pleasant, interesting person to have with you at any time. He's _____.

(b) She thinks she's socially superior. She looks down on others. She's a _____.

(c) He's very strict and correct. I think he doesn't like other people to enjoy themselves. He's a _____.

(d) She's always the first to arrive at a party. If the party's due to start at seven, she's there on the dot, or earlier. She's an _____.

(e) He likes to spend a lot of time alone. He's not keen on parties and usually does things on his own. He's a _____.

(f) She goes on and on telling people about her children, her house, her job, her opinions. . . I could go to sleep. She's a _____.

(g) She's very rich and spends her time between grand social occasions and luxury holidays in different parts of the world. She's a _____.

(h) He's always borrowing money and asking help from other people. He's a _____.

(i) He's an upper-class person and he's often seen at high-society parties and other social events. He's a _____.

(j) She's always causing difficulties for other people by interfering in their lives. She's a _____.

4 What type or types of person from the list at the top of the exercise above . . .

(a) . . . is extroverted?
(b) . . . is introverted?
(c) . . . might be class-conscious?
(d) . . . do you find interesting?
(e) . . . would get on well together? (make pairs, e.g. socialite and snob)
(f) . . . are you?

Sounds

1 Put the most suitable sound from the following list into each sentence below.

drone	**gasp**	**yell**	**chant**	**moan**
snort	**scream**	**whimper**	**boo**	**cheer**

(a) I heard the _____ of a terrified woman.
(b) He gave a tired _____ of pain.
(c) The Queen's arrival was met with an enthusiastic _____ from the crowd.
(d) The referee made another unpopular decision and the football crowd began to _____.
(e) When demonstrators march through the streets, they often _____ political slogans.
(f) He gave a _____ of surprise when he found the shower was ice-cold.
(g) The taxi-driver gave a _____ of contempt at the small tip.
(h) He used to _____ on and on monotonously and some of his listeners went to sleep listening to him.
(i) The little baby began to _____ weakly.
(j) I had to _____ at the top of my voice to make him hear me above the noise.

2 Which sounds from the list at the top of the exercise above . . .

(a) . . . can express pain?
(b) . . . can express disapproval?
(c) . . . can express surprise?

(d) . . . are loud?
(e) . . . are quiet?
(f) . . . are more normally associated with men?
(g) . . . are more normally associated with women?
(h) . . . might also be made by machines?
(i) . . . are often heard at football matches?
(j) . . . might be heard in a demonstration?
(k) . . . might come from a theatre audience?
(l) . . . can you make?

3 Instructions as in Exercise 1.

pop	**sizzle**	**thud**	**hiss**	**blare**
tinkle	**clink**	**swish**	**toll**	**chime**

(a) The great bell began to _____ sadly, solemnly, rhythmically.
(b) Some clocks _____ every hour.
(c) Tiny bells _____ in the wind.
(d) The heavy object fell to the ground with a _____.
(e) I love to hear the _____ of eggs and bacon frying in the pan.
(f) The peace and quiet was shattered when someone's radio began to _____ out.
(g) I heard a _____ from the tyre and knew I had a puncture.
(h) His sword stroke missed me by half an inch and I heard a _____ as it passed my nose.
(i) The ice-cube dropped into the empty glass with a _____.
(j) The cork finally came out of the bottle of champagne with a loud _____.

4 Which sounds from the list at the top of the exercise above . . .

(a) . . . do you consider pleasant?
(b) . . . do you consider unpleasant?
(c) . . . are made by bells?
(d) . . . are loud?
(e) . . . are quiet?
(f) . . . are often heard in a house?
(g) . . . are often heard at a party?
(h) . . . can you make?

5 Instructions as in Exercise 1.

plop	**boom**	**squelch**	**murmur**
hoot	**rattle**	**squeak**	**rumble**
chirrup	**click**		

(a) I heard a _____ as he put his foot into the deep, wet mud.
(b) The small stone dropped into the water with a quiet _____.
(c) The heavy old metal cart began to _____ over the stony road.
(d) I heard a loud _____ as the cannon fired.
(e) There is no more joyous sound than the _____ of bird-song.
(f) I can hear a _____. Something in your car needs oiling.
(g) I heard the _____ of rolling thunder in the distance.
(h) There was a small _____ as he closed the car-door.
(i) The impatient motorist began to _____ at the slow car in front.
(j) From my house you can hear the gentle _____ of a stream.

6   Which sounds from the list at the top of the exercise above . . .

(a) . . . do you consider pleasant?
(b) . . . do you consider unpleasant?
(c) . . . do you associate with the town?
(d) . . . do you associate with the country?
(e) . . . are loud?
(f) . . . are quiet?
(g) . . . are made by machines?
(h) . . . can describe the way people speak?
(i) . . . can be made by animals or birds?
(j) . . . can you make?

7   The onomatopoeic words in this exercise are usually used as nouns,
e.g. The constant *tap-tap-tap* of typewriters drove him mad. Match each
sound on the left below with an item on the right.

(a) ding-dong	iron gates closing
(b) tick-tock	violin-string breaking
(c) twang	wood fire burning
(d) clang	large bell
(e) toot-toot	car braking at speed
(f) bleep	car horn
(g) bang	clock
(h) pitter-patter	horses' hoofs on road
(i) crackle	light rain on window
(j) screech	bath-water going down plug-hole
(k) clip-clop	electronic personal caller
(l) gurgle	gun
(m) ping	spoon tapping empty wine-glass

Space Travel

Put each of the following words and phrases in its correct space below.

orbit	**splashdown**	**astronaut**	**mission**
dock	**countdown**	**launching pad**	**gravity**
launch	**spacecraft**	**lift-off**	**manned**

The first rockets to go into space carried no living creatures, but later
ones had mice or even dogs on them to see how (a) _____ (or rather
the lack of it) would affect them. The first (b) _____ space-flight took
place in 1962 and the first (c) _____ was the American, Alan
Shepherd. Everything at the (d) _____ was checked and ready as he
walked out to take his place in the rocket. Thousands of people had
come to watch the (e) _____ and they were silent as the final (f) _____
began: 10, 9, 8, 7, 6, 5, 4, 3, 2, 1, zero – (g) _____! The enormous
object raised itself into the sky and began its historic journey, to
(h) _____ safely in the ocean four hours later. Since then great
progress has been made. Alan Shepherd simply went up and came
down again, but now (i) _____ can go into (j) _____ and circle the
earth for days or weeks, or two of them can (k) _____ in space,
enabling people to pass between them. Each (l) _____ extends man's
knowledge of space.

Sport

1 Match each sport on the left below with the place where it is played on the right.

(a)	football	a court
(b)	swimming	a course
(c)	golf	a court
(d)	athletics	a pool
(e)	tennis	a court
(f)	volley-ball	a pitch
(g)	basketball	a circuit
(h)	boxing	a rink
(i)	shooting	a track
(j)	skating	a track/course
(k)	car-racing	a range
(l)	(horse)race	a ring

2 Match each sport on the left below with two pieces of equipment on the right.

(a)	ice hockey	club/tee
(b)	archery	racket/net
(c)	golf	puck/stick
(d)	tennis	parallel bars/mat
(e)	badminton	saddle/handlebars
(f)	boxing	toboggan/goggles
(g)	car-racing	bow/arrows
(h)	horse-racing	helmet/steering-wheel
(i)	cycling	épée/mask
(j)	shooting	whip/reins
(k)	winter sports	racket/shuttlecock
(l)	gymnastics	gloves/gumshield
(m)	fencing	rifle/target

3 In what sports are the following phrases heard and what do they mean?

(a) They're off!
(b) Seconds out!
(c) Fore!
(d) It's a foul, ref!
(e) Forty – love
(f) On your marks. . . Get set. . .
(g) Three – nil
(h) A bull's-eye!
(i) Four faults.

Time

1 Put each of the following words or phrases in its correct space in the sentences below.

turn of the century	**time zones**	**spell**
the small hours	**century**	**era**
chronological	**digital**	
local time	**decade**	

(a) Her parties usually finish before midnight, but sometimes they go on into _____.

(b) People who have _____ watches tend to say '7.50' rather than '10 to 8'.

(c) The plane is due to reach Bangkok at 5.30 a.m. _____.

(d) If you cross Russia, you pass through eight different _____.

(e) Novels don't always describe events in _____ order. It can be confusing.

(f) The First World War took place in the second _____ of this _____.

(g) After leaving university he had a _____ of teaching and then went into industry.

(h) In British history the period 1837 to 1901 is known as the Victorian _____.

(i) But that happened at the _____! It was more than 85 years ago!

2 Explain the difference between the items in each of the following pairs.

(a) dawn and dusk
(b) a month and a calendar month
(c) a year and a leap year

Tools and Equipment

1 Match each occupation on the left below with the most appropriate tool or piece of equipment on the right.

(a) doctor	a rake
(b) gardener	a hose
(c) jockey	a plane
(d) chef	an axe
(e) fireman	a baton
(f) lumberjack	a stethoscope
(g) conductor	a rolling pin
(h) blacksmith	an anchor
(i) carpenter	a whip
(j) photographer	a spanner
(k) mechanic	an exposure meter
(l) sailor	an anvil

2 Instructions as above.

(a)	violinist	a scalpel
(b)	window cleaner	a truncheon
(c)	fisherman	a pneumatic drill
(d)	tailor	a bucket
(e)	surgeon	a bow
(f)	usherette	a tape measure
(g)	policeman	a net
(h)	bricklayer	a spade
(i)	hairdresser	a compass
(j)	labourer	a torch
(k)	road mender	a trowel
(l)	navigator	a drier

3 Instructions as above.

(a)	disc jockey	radar
(b)	frogman	a briefcase
(c)	businessman	a turntable
(d)	librarian	a parking meter
(e)	office cleaner	flippers
(f)	air traffic controller	scaffolding
(g)	builder	a vacuum cleaner
(h)	traffic warden	a palette
(i)	undertaker	a crane
(j)	architect	a catalogue
(k)	artist	a hearse
(l)	docker	blueprints

4 Instructions as above.

(a)	a musician	a last
(b)	drugs detective	a clapperboard
(c)	weaver	a score
(d)	football referee	a kiln
(e)	shoemaker	a drill
(f)	telephone operator	a sniffer dog
(g)	farmer	a loom
(h)	potter	a filing cabinet
(i)	secretary	a whistle
(j)	film director	a till
(k)	dentist	a plough
(l)	cashier	headphones

Water

1 Put each word or phrase from the following list in its correct space in the sentences below.

current	ebb and flow	river bed	lock
estuary	river bank	tide	tributary
source			

(a) The beginning of a river is called its _____ and the wide mouth at the sea is its _____.

(b) A strong movement of water in the sea or river is a _____.

(c) Normally the sea is high or low according to the _____ of the _____.

(d) A smaller river which runs into a bigger one is called a _____.

(e) The bottom of the river is the _____ and on each side is the _____.

(f) The place on a river or canal where a pair of gates enables boats to change from one level to another is a _____.

2 Match each type of rain or fog on the left below with its definition on the right.

(a) sleet — continuous light rain

(b) mist — moisture found on grass at dawn

(c) drizzle — frozen rain falling as bits of ice

(d) smog — mixture of rain and snow

(e) hail — light fog at seashore or on river

(f) dew — mixture of smoke and fog

3 Put each word from the following list in its correct space in the sentences below.

water	meander	irrigate	flow
soak	trickle	dribble	splash
drip	spill	squirt	pour

(a) A tear began to _____ down her cheek.

(b) Be careful with that glass of water. It's very full. Don't _____ it.

(c) As a boy, I had a water-pistol which I used to _____ at my friends.

(d) When the new dam is completed, it will be possible to _____ an enormous area and make it fertile agricultural land.

(e) If you don't _____ your indoor plants regularly, they'll die.

(f) The bathroom tap wouldn't turn off properly and all night I could hear it _____.

(g) The road is under two inches of water. Don't stand near the edge of the pavement or the cars will _____ you.

(h) Let me _____ you a drink. Wine? Beer?

(i) When the baby tries to drink anything, she starts to _____ and we have to wipe her mouth.

(j) If your clothes are really dirty, _____ them in warm soapy water for an hour before you wash them.

(k) As a young river descends from the mountains, it will _____ in a straight line down the slope, but when it reaches the flat plain, it will slow down and _____ in wide turns to left and right.

WORD FORMATION

Word Forms

Fill each space in the sentences below with the correct form of the word in bold print above it.

E.g.   **decide**

       (a) We must come to a _____ very soon.
       (b) We beat them _____. We won 7:0.
       (c) He can never make up his mind. He's very _____.

Answers: (a) decision
          (b) decisively
          (c) indecisive

1 beauty
(a) She is very _____.
(b) She's training to be a _____.
(c) They're going to _____ the town with more trees and parks.

2 pay
(a) To buy this car I made a monthly _____ of £280 for two years.
(b) Please make your cheque _____ to John Watson.
(c) The person a cheque is made out to is called the _____.

3 receive
(a) She works as a _____ at a hotel in Scotland.
(b) Ask for a _____ when you buy something, in case you need to return it.
(c) I made several suggestions to improve production, but the management was not very _____ to my ideas.

4 hero
(a) He received a medal for his _____.
(b) They fought _____ in the war.
(c) She was described as a _____.

5 produce
(a) _____ of the new sports car has been halted by a strike.
(b) China is one of the world's leading _____ of rice.
(c) I'm afraid the talks were totally _____. We didn't reach agreement on anything.

6 explain
(a) An _____ leaflet is given to all purchasers of the machine.
(b) His disappearance is very strange, in fact quite _____.
(c) I think you owe me an _____ for your behaviour.

7 compare
(a) This is _____ better than that. In fact, there is really no _____.
(b) Scientists have made _____ tests on the new drugs.

8 advise
(a) Until the situation has settled down, it is _____ to travel to that country.
(b) The government set up an _____ body on the use of drugs in sport.
(c) I doubt the _____ of drinking alcohol while undergoing that medical treatment.

9 admire

(a) She was a pleasant, attractive girl, always surrounded by _____.
(b) I am full of _____ for what she has achieved.
(c) I approve of him wholeheartedly. He is an _____ man.

10 stable

(a) To _____ the boat in rough sea, we redistributed the weight.
(b) Between 1860 and 1900 the country had a number of revolutions and uprisings. It was a time of great _____.
(c) The exchange rate is going up and down dramatically. It's very _____ at the moment.

11 economy

(a) We're spending too much. We must _____.
(b) This car uses a lot of petrol. It's terribly _____.
(c) The Chancellor (Minister of Finance) is responsible for _____ affairs.

12 reside

(a) Buckingham Palace is the Queen's official _____ in London.
(b) There's no industry or entertainment here. It's a _____ district.
(c) All _____ of the neighbouring houses were warned of the gas leak.

13 comfort

(a) In that tense situation I found the good news very _____.
(b) I felt rather _____, so I put a soft cushion behind me.
(c) She sat in terrible _____ on the hard chair for over an hour.

14 dead

(a) The increasing number of _____ in traffic accidents is alarming.
(b) Be careful! That's a _____ poison!
(c) The doctor gave him an injection to _____ the pain.

15 demonstrate

(a) The _____ marched through the streets chanting slogans.
(b) Grandfather rarely showed the affection he felt for his family. He was a very _____ person.
(c) What you say is _____ false. Let me show you the facts.

16 imitate

(a) The bag is made of _____ leather.
(b) Small children are very _____ in their behaviour. They just copy what they see.
(c) His acting style is _____. No one can copy him.

17 argue

(a) She had an _____ with her husband last night.
(b) He's a very bad-tempered, _____ chap. He's always quarrelling.
(c) She is _____ the finest pianist in the world.

18 repeat

(a) He lost his temper and used disgusting, _____ language.
(b) In this essay you've said the same thing several times. It's very _____.
(c) I hope there will be no _____ of this shocking behaviour.

19 fail

(a) She is very efficient, and _____ polite to the customers.
(b) He considered himself a _____. He had succeeded in nothing.
(c) It was difficult to see much in the _____ light.

20 courage
(a) His friends tried to _____ him from attempting the dangerous climb.
(b) She _____ stood in the way of the escaping robbers.
(c) His parents gave him a lot of _____ in his studies.

21 real
(a) I think it's a bit _____ to hope that world peace can be gained so easily.
(b) He spends all his time in romantic daydreams. He's lost touch with _____.
(c) Ladies and gentlemen, I am a _____ and I think we must face facts.

22 false
(a) She was accused of _____ the financial accounts.
(b) It is a _____ to say he did it when you know he didn't.
(c) The _____ of his argument was obvious to everyone.

23 prophesy
(a) I am not a _____ and I would not like to make a _____ on whether the world can survive this age of nuclear weapons.
(b) What he wrote in 1930 was _____. Much of what he described has come true.

24 describe
(a) The damage caused by the earthquake cannot be imagined. It was _____.
(b) The teacher asked them to write a _____ passage about their home towns.
(c) The witness was able to give a full _____ of the wanted man.

25 friend
(a) The _____ between the two soon developed into love.
(b) In London she was _____ by a rich woman who looked after her and helped her.
(c) The desert is a dangerous, _____ place.

26 sense
(a) He felt a strange, painful _____ in his back.
(b) Even the most _____ person ought to appreciate the beauty of this music.
(c) What an idiotic, _____ thing to do!

27 famous
(a) The _____ of the Beatles soon spread outside Britain.
(b) The day of the massacre will go down in history as a terrible, _____ day. It was a day of _____.

28 defend
(a) I just want to ask you a few ordinary questions, so why don't you relax? Why are you so _____?
(b) The government's policy on arms is shocking. It is quite _____.
(c) We must do all we can for the _____ of this nation against possible attack.

29 agree
(a) What an unpleasant, _____ old woman she is!
(b) We finally reached _____ on the matter at midnight.
(c) I liked the place. I found the people, the weather and the food very _____.

30 possess
(a) In his will he left all his money and _____ to his wife.
(b) She was a very _____ mother. She gave her son very little freedom.
(c) The actor playing the main part should be the _____ of a very good voice, good looks and a very strong physique.

31 different
(a) I'm afraid I have to _____. I don't agree with you at all.
(b) Politeness is one thing. Real kindness is another. You must learn to _____ between the two.
(c) We get along pretty well, although of course we have our _____ from time to time.

32 active
(a) The firm maintained that the strike was organized by a group of political _____.
(b) The fire-prevention system is _____ by any small increase in temperature.
(c) It is quite safe to go near the volcano. It has been _____ for years.

33 form
(a) It is especially important for children to have love and affection in their _____ years.
(b) The slight _____ in his left hand was corrected by surgery.
(c) The police are considering the _____ of a new anti-drugs unit.

34 compel
(a) Military service is no longer _____ in Britain.
(b) Membership of the Students' Club is entirely voluntary. There is no _____ whatsoever.
(c) All staff should attend the meeting. Only the most _____ reasons for absence will be accepted.

35 enthusiasm
(a) They threw themselves _____ into the new project.
(b) He's a real golf _____. He loves the game.
(c) They didn't really _____ over my idea. In fact there was some opposition.

36 create
(a) Ian Fleming, the _____ of James Bond, died in 1964.
(b) Although she is very able technically, she isn't _____ enough for this kind of work.
(c) The _____ of the North Atlantic Treaty Organization took place in 1949.

37 necessary
(a) We regret that the present economic difficulties will _____ a reduction in our work force.
(b) I sympathize with his point of view, but I don't always _____ agree with him.
(c) He lives very simply, with just the basic _____ of life.

38 destroy

(a) The control centre is deep underground and completely _____ except by a direct hit from a nuclear missile.

(b) War plans include the immediate _____ of all enemy military bases.

(c) His criticism of my work was entirely _____. There was nothing useful or constructive in it at all.

39 manage

(a) Talks between workers and _____ have broken down and a strike now seems unavoidable.

(b) The boy was very violent and his parents found him _____.

(c) To improve his qualifications he's taking a course in _____ skills.

40 believe

(a) It was an incredible story, quite _____.

(b) She is a person of very strong religious _____.

(c) His explanation was obviously false and the judge made no attempt to hide his _____.

Portmanteau Words

Certain English words are formed by combining parts of two words, often the first part of one and the last part of another (e.g. 'smog' is a combination of 'smoke' and 'fog') and sometimes the two first parts (e.g. a 'moped' is a 'motorized, pedal-assisted bicycle'). Explain the meanings of the following 'portmanteau' words and then put each in its correct sentence below.

Swatch	**brunch**	**motel**	**Oxfam**
bedsit	**Oxbridge**	**Interpol**	**Eurovision**
Chunnel			

(a) The _____ Song Contest is watched by millions of viewers from Portugal to Finland, from Greece to Iceland, and in other countries.

(b) The _____ organization, which has the aim of relieving hunger throughout the world, was founded in Oxford.

(c) The International Police Commission, with headquarters in Paris, is usually referred to as _____.

(d) If you get up late at the week-end, you might decide to have _____ in the middle of the morning.

(e) The British and French governments have taken the first steps towards building a _____ to link the two countries.

(f) After driving all day, we looked for a cheap, clean _____ to stop at for the night.

(g) In the past a university degree from _____ was a great advantage to anyone wanting a career in the diplomatic service.

(h) There's a certain kind of Swiss watch called a _____.

(i) She can't afford a proper flat. She rents a _____.

Prefixes

1 **arch-** (chief, main, highest-ranking) **out-** (more, better etc. than) **mal-** (badly, wrongly) **pseudo-** (false, pretended)

Put each of the above prefixes in its correct space in the sentences below.

(a) In my opinion this book is just _____-intellectual rubbish.
(b) Although he was older than his wife, he _____lived her by ten years.
(c) Priests are not often ambitious men, but he had set his heart on becoming _____bishop.
(d) The launch of the space-rocket was delayed by a _____function in the fuel system.
(e) At the beginning of the nineteenth century, Britain's _____-enemy was France.
(f) He completely _____boxed his opponent and knocked him out in the seventh round.
(g) Children who grow up in time of war are more likely to be _____adjusted than other children.
(h) He uses _____-scientific language to persuade his readers.
(i) These squalid, dark, cramped, _____odorous rooms are homes to whole families of people.
(j) She was the finest dancer in the country. She _____shone all the others.

2 Explain the meanings of the following words and phrases.

(a) a pseudonym
(b) arch-rivals
(c) maladministration
(d) out-size clothes
(e) malnutrition
(f) pseudo-religious
(g) an arch-villain
(h) to outstay your welcome

3 **a-** (not, without) **hyper-** (extremely, too)
fore- (before, in front of) **neo-** (new, revived)

(a) The British Museum was built in the middle of the last century in the _____-classical style popular at that time.
(b) Who can _____tell what the future holds for us?
(c) It's no use asking him about the political system or the parties. He doesn't know or care. He's completely _____political.
(d) It's quite normal to complain if you think something is wrong, but I do feel that you are sometimes _____critical.
(e) The authorities are concerned at the activities of a small _____-Nazi movement.
(f) You must be very careful what you say about her poems. She's a _____sensitive person.
(g) She didn't know the difference between right and wrong. She had no conscience at all. She was simply _____moral.
(h) The police claimed that she had some _____knowledge of the murder attempt and could have prevented it.
(i) He was standing in the middle, in the _____ground of the picture.
(j) Young children can sometimes be _____active, which means that they can't keep still.

4 Explain the meanings of the following words and phrases.

(a) neo-imperialism
(b) an atheist
(c) a foretaste
(d) a hypermarket

(e) hypertension
(f) a foregone conclusion
(g) an asymmetrical shape
(h) a neo-Fascist

5 **uni-, mono-** (one) **duo-, bi-** (two) **tri-** (three)
quad-, quart- (four) **pent-, quin-** (five) **sex-** (six)
sept- (seven) **oct-** (eight) **non-** (nine) **dec-** (ten)
cent- (hundred)

Complete the words in the passage below.

George Willis was born in 1900 and was too young to go into
uni_____ in the First World War, which took place in the second
dec_____ of the cent_____. Instead he finished his schooling and
went to university. Like most Oxford colleges, his college was built
round a quad_____ and a photograph of him there shows him
wearing a mono_____ in his eye, one of his many eccentricities. He
rode a tri_____, declaring it to be safer and more stable than a
bi_____. His subject was zoology. Initially he studied bi_____, but
soon tired of two-legged creatures and took an interest in quad_____,
developing a special affection for elephants. However, all animal life
fascinated him and he was often to be seen in the Oxfordshire
countryside, observing wildlife through his bi_____ or setting up his
tri_____ to record it in photographs. Marine creatures also attracted
him, especially, for some reason, the oct_____. He was also creative
in such diverse fields as engineering (he proposed a scheme for
mono_____ transport in London) and music (he formed a jazz
sex_____, which later became a quin_____ when the drummer
joined the navy, a quar_____ when the violinist was run over by a
bus and a tri_____ when the trombonist was imprisoned for
bi_____). He travelled widely and spoke French so well that he was
completely bi_____. He was a fine sportsman and won many prizes
in the pent_____. In 1972, although by this time a sept_____, he
wrote his first play, a strange piece which consisted of a duo_____
between Shakespeare and Churchill. He is still active and talkative,
although conversations with him tend to be mono_____. He talks and
others listen. Always optimistic, he looks forward to continuing his busy
life as a non_____ and to becoming a cent_____. He lives with his
wife, a lively oct_____, and has two sons and a daughter, whose
birth as tri_____ in 1927 he describes as the happiest event in his
eventful life.

6 Explain the meanings of the following words.

(a) bicentenary
(b) pentagon
(c) centenary
(d) tricolour
(e) monotonous
(f) decathlon
(g) sexagenarian
(h) quintuplets

(i) bisect
(j) cent
(k) biplane
(l) bicameral
(m) unicycle
(n) quadruplets
(o) unicorn

Suffixes

1 **-phobia** (fear or hatred of)   **-cide** (killer, killing)   **-gamy** (marriage)

Put each of the above suffixes in its correct place in the sentences below.

(a) Those rose-bushes need protection. Spray them with insecti_____.
(b) He gets very tense and nervous in enclosed spaces like lifts and the underground. He suffers from claustro_____.
(c) The custom of having more than one wife or husband is known as 'poly_____'.
(d) Some people, and some animals, are terrified of water. This aversion is known as aqua_____.
(e) His problems overwhelmed him and he finally comitted sui_____.
(f) When he was arrested and charged with bi_____, both his wives stood by him.
(g) His Anglo_____ comes from some bad experiences he had in England.
(h) Following the man's death, his wife was charged with homi_____.

2 Explain the meanings of the following words and phrases.

(a) germicide
(b) xenophobia
(c) patricide
(d) a monogamous society
(e) fratricide
(f) agoraphobia

3 **-maniac** (obsessed person)   **-phile** (lover of)
-monger (dealer in)

Instructions as above.

(a) A person who makes and exploits war is called a war_____.
(b) He has always been a biblio_____ and has amassed a vast collection of books over the years.
(c) He has a shop selling pots and pans, tools and other metal goods. He's an iron_____.
(d) He's unbelievably self-centred and arrogant. He's a complete ego_____.
(e) She loved the year she spent in Italy and has been an Italo_____ ever since.
(f) Some journalists are perfectly honest and well-meaning but she just makes a profit from gossip and rumour. She's just a cheap scandal_____.
(g) A klepto_____ is a person who has a compulsive desire to steal.
(h) His fondness for drink became an addiction, and his doctor says he is now a dipso_____.

4 Explain the meanings of the following words and phrases.

(a) a pyromaniac
(b) Francophilia
(c) a fishmonger
(d) an Anglophile
(e) a mania
(f) a film maniac

5 **-worthy** (deserving, fit for) **-like** (similar to) **-most** (furthest)

(a) To me, at 14, the film-stars I saw at my local cinema were god_____ creatures.

(b) John O'Groats in Scotland is the northern_____ town in mainland Britain.

(c) We are pleased to present you with this award for your praise_____ work among the poor of this city.

(d) In the old days it was not considered lady_____ for a woman to smoke in public, if at all.

(e) Architecture during that period was very boring. Almost every building was a box-_____ structure, with no variation or decoration to please the eye.

(f) We're looking for an honest, reliable, trust_____ person to handle our legal affairs.

(g) He betrayed the inner_____ secrets of his country's government to the enemy.

(h) A small accident like that won't appear in the papers. It isn't news_____ enough.

6 Explain the meanings of the following phrases.

(a) a business-like manner
(b) his foremost thought
(c) a roadworthy car
(d) a noteworthy comment
(e) a life-like statue
(f) outermost defences

7 **-wards** (in the direction of) **-esque** (like, in the manner of) **-some** (causing, making)

(a) I have a backache which is a bit trouble_____ at times.

(b) He cast his eyes heaven_____ as if imploring God for help or pity.

(c) It's very pictur_____ here, with the trees attractively framing the view of the river.

(d) From Colombia we went south_____ through Ecuador, Peru and Bolivia to Argentina.

(e) Man's first view of the earth from space was an awe_____ sight.

(f) The back garden faces sea_____ so you can always be sure of a pleasant view.

(g) I'm afraid I find her constant chatter gets a bit weari_____ after a while.

(h) The architecture here is rather Roman_____. Look at the round arches and thick walls.

8 Explain the meanings of the following phrases.

(a) quarrelsome boys
(b) outwardly confident
(c) a statuesque figure
(d) a downward movement
(e) a tiresome person
(f) a Kafkaesque novel

9 -scape (scenery)   **-scope** (means of observing)
-ette, -let, -ling (small)

(a) Even the most powerful tele_____ does not make the smallest
   stars visible.
(b) I watched a drop_____ of rain move slowly down the window.
(c) His most famous sea_____ was painted in 1879 and hangs in the
   National Gallery.
(d) A gos_____ is a young goose.
(e) The award takes the form of a silver statu_____ of the Greek god,
   Adonis.
(f) The first television picture of the hitherto mysterious moon_____
   was the most dramatic sight I have ever seen.
(g) His home is in the country and he's wondering if he can afford to
   buy a flat_____ in London too.
(h) The crew of a submarine just below the surface can see what is
   happening above by looking through the peri_____.
(i) Travelling by car, you have the chance to stop in the countryside to
   admire the land_____.

10 Explain the meanings of the following words and phrases.

(a) a microscopic insect
(b) a piglet
(c) a duckling
(d) a kitchenette
(e) a marvellous cloudscape
(f) a booklet

11 -ist

Make sentences by connecting each person on the left below with the
correct phrase on the right.

(a) An ornithologist	speaks many languages.
(b) A philatelist	performs post-mortems on dead bodies.
(c) A feminist	is interested in birds.
(d) A numismatist	writes plays.
(e) A philanthropist	sets fire to property.
(f) A pathologist	is interested in stamps.
(g) A linguist	stuffs dead animals.
(h) A dramatist	is interested in coins.
(i) A seismologist	believes in equal rights for women.
(j) A manicurist	hates women.
(k) A pharmacist	is an expert on China.
(l) A meteorologist	gives large amounts of money to charity.
(m) An arsonist	is an expert on earthquakes.
(n) A taxidermist	makes up medicines.
(o) A misogynist	looks after people's feet.
(p) A somnambulist	looks after people's hands and fingernails.
(q) A Sinologist	is a handwriting expert.
(r) A chiropodist	studies the weather.
(s) A graphologist	walks in his or her sleep.

Compound Adjectives

Rewrite each of the sentences below, forming a compound adjective from the two words in italics and making any other changes necessary.

E.g.   The journey took *ten hours*.
        They *make* these chocolates by *hand*.
        Her hat *caught* everyone's *eye*.
        The doctor was *trained* in *Germany*.
        The memory was both *bitter* and *sweet*.

Answers: It was a *ten-hour* journey.
        These chocolates are *hand-made*.
        She wore an *eye-catching* hat.
        He's a *German-trained* doctor.
        It was a *bitter-sweet* memory.

1
(a) That thing *looks dangerous*.
(b) Mr Reed is an accountant who was *born* in *London*.
(c) She always *dresses* very *smartly*.
(d) It was painted *red* like the colour of *bricks*.
(e) She had eyes *like* a *cat*.
(f) It was an occasion which was *happy* and *sad* at the same time.
(g) The tower has a *shape* like a *mushroom*.
(h) He was *famous* all over the *world*.
(i) We had to write a composition of *200 words*.

2
(a) The meal *tasted awful*.
(b) Only planes with a *single engine* can land here.
(c) A building of *five storeys* suddenly collapsed.
(d) We walked along a corridor which had a *red carpet*.
(e) This machine is *operated* by *hand*.
(f) The new director is an economist *educated* at *Oxford*.
(g) He has very *broad shoulders*.
(h) She's always very *satisfied* with *herself*.
(i) My sister is very *conscious* of *dress*.

3
(a) We'll have a guide who *speaks French*.
(b) The walls were as *blue* as the *sky*.
(c) I looked at the sea, which was rather *blue* but also rather *green*.
(d) The ship sailed with a crew of *eight men*.
(e) She had *fair hair*.
(f) The new machinery, *built* in *America*, will arrive next month.
(g) I heard a voice that *sounded strange*.
(h) These tigers *eat men*.
(i) He always has a *bad temper*.

4
(a) The experiment was done with balloons *filled* with *gas*.
(b) My teenage son is *mad* about *football*.
(c) I'm afraid my wife *spends* very *freely*.
(d) He certainly has *good intentions*.
(e) They have very *bad manners*.
(f) The firm has its *base* in *New York*.

(g) Those cars are a very *high price*.
(h) The noise *split* our *ears*!
(i) I need a car with *four doors*.

Noun Plurals

1 Put the words in brackets into the sentences, in the same order, in their plural forms.

(a) A large number of _____ fled in fear when a flock of _____ suddenly landed within a few _____ of them. (mouse, goose, foot)

(b) Automobile _____ have all too many _____ of _____ in _____ of the special security _____ and are considering _____ of manufacturing their own. (company, story, delay, delivery, key, way)

(c) Security _____ believe the _____ climbed along the _____ of several houses before forcing open an upper window of the office building with _____ and escaping with the contents of two _____. (chief, thief, roof, knife, safe)

(d) With the help of old _____, war-time Paris was recreated in the film _____ for the film '_____ of War', in which all the _____ were played by unknown actors. (photo, studio, echo, hero)

(e) _____ were surprised when no fewer than six _____ in full uniform, carrying _____, arrived in _____ to attend a series of _____. (passer-by, commander-in-chief, brief-case, police car, court-martial)

(f) The _____ and _____ in the park are sometimes alarmed by low-flying _____. (deer, sheep, aircraft)

2 Put the words in brackets into the sentences in their plural forms.

(a) The government has been faced with a number of _____ recently. (crisis)

(b) It was one of the most beautiful _____ in France. (chateau)

(c) He irritated his staff by sending them a constant stream of _____. (memorandum)

(d) Scientists are now doing _____ of the various substances. (analysis)

(e) The number of travel _____ in the city gets bigger every year. (bureau)

(f) They had to drill through many different rock _____ before they found oil. (stratum)

(g) Students are reminded that their _____ must be handed in by the end of term. (thesis)

(h) Astronomers have noticed a number of strange _____ in the sky recently. (phenomenon)

(i) Different people make different judgements because of their differing _____. (criterion)

(j) Television, radio and the press are often collectively referred to as the mass _____. (medium)

PROBLEM WORDS

Confusing Word Pairs

Choose the correct word for each space.

1 **misused** (badly, wrongly used)
   disused (no longer used)

   (a) An airport _____ since its closure ten years before was used for car-racing.
   (b) They complained that the new law had been _____ to suppress individual liberties.
   (c) Be careful of this word. It is often _____.
   (d) The goods were stored in a _____ cinema.

2 **unreadable** (too boring or too badly written to read)
   illegible (physically impossible to read)

   (a) His hand-writing is so bad it's _____.
   (b) The book is long, uninteresting and not very well-written. I find it
       _____.
   (c) After years of being exposed to the sun and rain, the sign over the shop had become completely _____.
   (d) I think her novels are _____. The style is awful and the plots are ridiculous.

3 **dependent** (depending)
   dependant (person who depends on another for home, money, food)

   (a) The signing of the contract is _____ on whether you can guarantee delivery of the goods within three months.
   (b) You are entitled to receive a government allowance for each _____ who is living with you.
   (c) This residence document permits you, but no _____, to live and work in this country.
   (d) The empire consisted of the kingdom and all its _____ colonies.

4 **story** (tale, plot)
   storey (floor or level in building)

   (a) I live in a flat on the seventh _____.
   (b) I'll tell you a _____.
   (c) The basic _____ of the novel is rather weak but it's amusing and well-written.
   (d) They're putting up a new 20-_____ hotel on this site.

5 **historic** (important in history)
   historical (concerning history)

   (a) At the meeting of our local _____ society there will be a talk on 'France in the 19th Century'.
   (b) Today we have gained our independence and our liberty. It is a _____ day for our country.
   (c) She likes _____ novels, especially romances set in the 16th and 17th centuries.
   (d) In 1945 there was a _____ meeting of world leaders which changed the course of world events.

6 immigration (coming into a country to settle)
  emigration (leaving a country to settle elsewhere)

  (a) If we don't restrict _____ into this country, the pressure on our social services will be intolerable.
  (b) When times were hard in Britain, there was very large _____ to Australia and Canada.

7 draft (rough preliminary version, to make a rough preliminary version)
  draught (i: current of cold air in a room   ii: beer, not in bottles, straight from the barrel)

  (a) Don't sit there. You'll be in a _____. The window doesn't close properly.
  (b) The Prime Minister discussed with his secretary the _____ of the speech he was going to make the following day.
  (c) Some people prefer _____ beer. They say bottles give beer a different taste.
  (d) Lawyers were instructed to _____ a law for the consideration of the cabinet.

8 dissatisfied (discontented, displeased, not satisfied with quality)
  unsatisfied (unfulfilled, not satisfied with quantity)

  (a) He ate a meal large enough for three normal people but his appetite was still _____.
  (b) I'm very _____ with this computer. It keeps breaking down.
  (c) If you are _____ with the service, you should complain.
  (d) Demand for the new car is still _____ in spite of an increase in production.

9 suit (be suitable for)
  suite [swi:t] (group of things belonging together, set)

  (a) Will seven o'clock _____ you or shall I come later?
  (b) She took a _____ of rooms at the Bristol Hotel.
  (c) For the living-room we can either buy a complete _____ of matching furniture or get different items separately.
  (d) Do you think a dark brown overcoat would _____ me?

10 licence (document giving official permission to do something, *noun*)
  license (to give a licence, *verb*)

  (a) The annual _____ for a colour television set in Britain now costs over £60.
  (b) The authorities refused to _____ him to export arms.
  (c) He was _____d to sell alcohol, but after his court conviction, his _____ was cancelled.

11 prophecy (prediction, *noun*)
  prophesy (predict, *verb*)

  (a) I _____ that he will pass his exam and get a good job.
  (b) I will make a _____. There will be a new government in less than a year.

12 **device** (new invention, means of doing something, *noun*)
   devise (invent, *verb*)

   (a) Anyone who can _____ a means of recording television programmes without recording the advertisements will make a fortune.
   (b) He invented a _____ for warning pilots if there was bad weather ahead.
   (c) A _____ can be attached to a private telephone which keeps a record of all calls made and their cost.
   (d) He managed to _____ a system of bonus payments to encourage hard-working staff.

13 **goal** [gəʊl] (i: point won in football etc.   ii: aim, ambition)
   gaol [dʒeɪl] (prison, send to prison)

   (a) He scored the winning _____ of the match.
   (b) He spent eight years in _____ for armed robbery.
   (c) She finally achieved her _____ of becoming director of the firm.
   (d) The judge said he had no option but to _____ her.

14 **enquiry/enquiries** (request for information)
   inquiry/inquiries (formal investigation)

   (a) You should make _____ at the office.
   (b) Official _____ are always held after plane crashes.
   (c) We have received a number of _____ about our new product since putting an advertisement in the newspaper.
   (d) It was never discovered where the missing money went, in spite of a searching _____ by the bank.

15 **exhausting** (very tiring)
   exhaustive (very thorough, complete)

   (a) _____ tests were carried out to discover the cause of the plane's engine failure.
   (b) The older members of the group found the long journey quite _____.
   (c) He never stops talking. He's an _____ person to be with.
   (d) The police carried out an _____ investigation, but the missing woman was never found.

16 **disinterested** (impartial)
   uninterested (not interested, bored, apathetic)

   (a) Only 22% of the people voted. The rest were totally _____.
   (b) The management and the union asked a completely _____ party to mediate between them.
   (c) I don't know why he didn't go to the exhibition. Perhaps he was too busy or just _____.
   (d) France's intervention in the dispute was not entirely _____. It gave her increased power and influence in the area.

17 council (district government)
counsel (i: kind of lawyer in court   ii: to advise)

(a) The job of a Vocational Guidance Officer is to _____ young people on their careers.
(b) I have complained to the local _____ about the poor condition of the pavements.
(c) The prosecuting _____ demanded the death penalty but the judge gave her a life sentence.
(d) Some men from the _____ came to plant trees along the river.

18 councillor (member of a council)
counsellor (adviser)

(a) She and her husband often argued, so they went to a marriage _____ for help.
(b) He's always been interested in local government. Now he's been elected _____.

19 unknown (not known)
infamous (shameful, notorious)

(a) The show was such a success that she went from being an _____ actress to a star overnight.
(b) Joseph Jackson was an _____ mass-murderer of Victorian times.
(c) His action in cheating poor, sick and elderly people of their savings was described by the judge as _____.
(d) The firm was almost _____ ten years ago but now it is famous for its high-quality products.

20 certainly (definitely, really)
surely (expresses surprise, doubt, relief)

(a) _____ you aren't going out like that, are you?
(b) I am _____ not inviting Teresa to my party. I've never liked her.
(c) Your coat must be here somewhere, _____!
(d) He _____ impressed me. I thought he was very bright and talented.

21 dairy (i: place where milk is kept, butter, cheese etc. made; shop selling milk products   ii: related to milk products)
diary (daily record of events)

(a) He kept a _____ from the age of 15 to 21.
(b) We're still waiting for milk deliveries from the _____.
(c) No, we don't grow wheat or vegetables. It's a _____ farm. We have about 200 cows.
(d) She has a regular column in the *Daily News* describing the various activities of the day. It's called 'Annabel's _____.'

22 compliment (to praise, piece of praise)
complement (go together or combine well, add to)

(a) He lacks confidence and she is a strong person. They _____ each other very well.
(b) He paid her a nice _____ on her new dress.
(c) I'd like to _____ you on your performance. It was excellent.
(d) Weight-lifting gives strength. Running increases stamina. The two exercises _____ each other.

23 **first** (first item in list of reasons, actions etc.)
  at first (initial attitude before change)

  (a) _____ boil the water, then add salt, then put in the potatoes, then. . .
  (b) He found the job difficult _____, but soon got used to it.
  (c) _____ they didn't like their new boss.
  (d) _____ I phoned the police, then I made a list of what had been stolen, then I made myself a cup of tea.

24 **lastly** (final item in list of reasons, actions etc.)
  at last (final result)

  (a) The police questioned him for three hours until _____ he confessed.
  (b) . . . then stir the mixture in the saucepan, then leave for five minutes and _____ add sugar.
  (c) _____ I succeeded in making him understand!
  (d) There are several reasons why he's leaving the country. First, he hates the weather here, secondly, he can't find a good job, and _____, he's homesick.

Difficult Verb Pairs

A small number of verbs give problems because the past tense (and usually also the past participle) of one verb has the same spelling as the present tense and infinitive of the other. In each sentence below use the right form of the correct verb.

1 **fall, fell, fallen**
  fell, felled, felled (cut down)

  (a) Prices have _____ steeply since last August.
  (b) Three old trees will have to be _____ because they are diseased and dangerous.
  (c) He lost his balance and _____ heavily.

2 **find, found, found**
  found, founded, founded (establish)

  (a) My grandfather _____ this firm in 1924.
  (b) While clearing out the bedroom, I _____ these old letters.
  (c) The United Nations was _____ in 1945.

3 **bind, bound, bound** (tie up)
  bound, bounded, bounded (i: jump   ii: border)

  (a) Switzerland is _____ by France, Germany, Austria and Italy.
  (b) The lion _____ forward and sprang at her.
  (c) He was _____ hand and foot by the robbers.

4 see, saw, seen
saw, sawed, sawed/sawn (cut with a saw)

(a) I suddenly _____ a face at the window.
(b) He _____ the branch in half and put the pieces on the fire.
(c) Two prisoners _____ through the bars of their cell window and escaped.

5 grind, ground, ground (crush into powder)
ground, grounded, grounded (compel to remain on the ground)

(a) The ship went too near the coast and was _____ on rocks.
(b) The beans are _____ in this machine before they are put in the coffee pot.
(c) The airline has decided to _____ all its planes until special safety checks have been carried out.

6 wind, wound [waʊnd], wound (twist)
wound [wuːnd], wounded, wounded (injure)

(a) The train _____ its way up the hillside and stopped just below the top.
(b) The police opened fire and _____ six of the rioters.
(c) Keep still and I'll _____ a bandage round your arm.

7 lie, lay, lain (be or put oneself in a horizontal position, *intransitive*)
lay, laid, laid (put, *transitive*)

(a) He _____ the enormous box on the ground and looked for a taxi.
(b) He _____ there for an hour until someone finally heard his cries for help.
(c) In this school emphasis is _____ on discipline and hard work.
(d) I'm tired. I think I'll _____ down for a while.
(e) They were ordered to _____ down their weapons.
(f) The villages _____ at the foot of the mountains.

Some verbs have two past participle forms and there is usually no difference between the two (e.g. learned/learnt, sawed/sawn). However, in a few cases the two forms are used for two different applications of the verb and are not interchangeable. In each sentence below use the correct past participle form of the verb.

8 bear, bore, born (give birth to) borne (i: carry ii: endure)

(a) He was _____ in London in 1906.
(b) The winning team were _____ through the streets on the shoulders of their excited supporters.
(c) No-one else could have _____ the terrible experiences he went through.

9 load, loaded, loaded (put on for transport) laden (weigh down)

(a) The table was _____ with good things. It was a real feast.
(b) The ship has now been _____ and is ready to sail.
(c) The snow-_____ branches were drooping and at breaking point.

10 cost,   **cost, cost** (be of certain price)
                 costed, costed (calculate the cost of)

(a) Accountants and engineers have _____ a new heating system for the factory. The board of directors will consider their estimates and decide whether to go ahead with the scheme.
(b) Houses have never _____ more than they do today.
(c) The proposed new road system has been _____ by experts at £73,000,000.

11 hang,   **hung, hung** (suspend)
                 hanged, hanged (kill by hanging)

(a) When you've _____ your coat up, come and sit down.
(b) Before the abolition of the death penalty, convicted murderers were sometimes _____.
(c) This picture has been badly _____. It should be nearer the light and lower.

12 strike, struck,   **struck** (hit)
                        stricken (attack, e.g. with fear, doubt, disease)

(a) Thousands of people have been _____ by this terrible illness.
(b) I have never _____ anyone in my life.
(c) Panic-_____, they rushed through the flames to the exits.

Ambiguous Words

The following sentences have two different meanings, due to the ambiguity of the words in italics. Explain the two meanings of each sentence.

(a) She was driving on the *right* side of the road.
(b) He's very *fair*.
(c) She was a very *funny* girl.
(d) Half the workers in the factory are *idle*.
(e) They did not *recognize* the new President.
(f) She's a very *curious* person.
(g) It's a very *cheap* newspaper.
(h) They are *expected* to arrive at seven.
(i) My grandfather was a very *powerful* man.
(j) I thought he was rather *suspicious*.
(k) She was very *jealous* of her husband's reputation.
(l) She likes to *entertain* people.
(m) John *should* know the answer.
(n) He didn't *appeal* to me.
(o) The *Morning News* is a *popular* newspaper.
(p) He *might* have phoned.
(q) I'm afraid I'm not *prepared* to leave yet.
(r) The teacher *insisted* that his pupils did their homework regularly.
(s) He *took advantage* of his friend's knowledge.

False Friends

Speakers of other, mainly European, languages may come across certain English words and because they look similar to words in their own language wrongly assume that the meaning is the same. The confusion might be because of a chance similarity in spelling; because the original meaning, in one or other language, has changed over the years; or because the original word was borrowed from one language and, from the start, used differently in the other. Such words are called 'false friends'.

In each pair of words below, the first word is the false friend and the second is the word it is often confused with. Put each word in its correct place in the sentences which follow each pair.

1 **actual** (real)
   present (current, existing now)

   (a) Reagan and Nixon are former American Presidents. Who is the
       _____ one?
   (b) I've known many rich men, but he is the only _____ millionaire I've
       met.
   (c) She used to work in advertising, but her _____ job is in journalism.

2 **ignore** (deliberately take no notice of, pay no attention to)
   not know

   (a) His speech was interrupted by loud shouts but he wisely decided to
       _____ them and carry on.
   (b) How can you _____ your teacher's name? You see her every day!
   (c) Well, if you _____ my warnings, I cannot be responsible for what
       happens to you.

3 **formidable** (causing fear, difficult to achieve)
   wonderful

   (a) It was a _____ party. We all enjoyed ourselves very much.
   (b) To prepare for that difficult exam in only three months! That's a
       _____ task! I don't think I can do it.
   (c) The northern approaches to the city are protected by _____
       defences which only the strongest attack could penetrate.
   (d) She's a _____ person. Everyone likes and admires her.

4 **camping** (activity of holidaying in a tent)
   camp-site (place for setting up tents)

   (a) I like to go _____ in the summer.
   (b) We found a lovely _____ near the sea to put up our tent.

5 **morale** (spirits, state of mind)
   moral (right, proper, virtuous)

   (a) Regular mail and good food are important to maintain the _____ of
       soldiers during a war.
   (b) It was a good move financially, but from the _____ point of view I
       have my doubts.
   (c) As we became aware of the difficulties that lay ahead, our _____
       dropped.
   (d) He's a very _____ person who is guided by the highest principles.

6 **frequent** (go to often)
   attend (go to a school or course etc., be present at)

   (a) Please state the name and address of the college you _____.
   (b) Criminals are known to _____ the clubs and bars in this street.
   (c) Wild animals _____ the river bank at night and traps are set to catch them.
   (d) Delegates from twelve countries are expected to _____ the meeting.

7 **adequate** (enough, sufficient)
   suitable (right for the purpose)

   (a) Make sure you have _____ money for the trip. £50 should be enough.
   (b) I'll come at six, or any other _____ time you suggest.
   (c) Do you think this dress is _____ for tonight's party, or is it too formal?
   (d) Rice-growing can only be successful if there is _____ rainfall.

8 **argument** (i: disagreement   ii: supporting reason)
   subject (something talked or written about or studied)

   (a) My favourite _____ at school was geography.
   (b) He and his wife had a heated _____ about which car to buy.
   (c) The best _____ against smoking is its effect on health.
   (d) The _____ of the essay we had to write was 'World Peace'.

9 **eventually** (finally, after a long time)
   possibly (perhaps or maybe)

   (a) The Socialist Party will win, _____ with a majority of over fifty.
   (b) After travelling all day, they _____ reached home at midnight.
   (c) He's arriving on Tuesday, or _____ Wednesday.
   (d) At the moment he has only one shop, but he hopes to have a nationwide chain _____.

10 **dancing** (activity of dance)
   dance-hall (large room where people go to dance)

   (a) _____ is good exercise.
   (b) We went to a nice _____ in the town.

11 **experience** (i: previous knowledge or work   ii: event)
   experiment (test carried out to see result)

   (a) Meeting the President was an _____ I shall never forget.
   (b) We'll try an _____ with these chemicals and see what happens.
   (c) This is a very responsible job, so we want someone with a lot of _____.
   (d) The _____ of arranging the students' chairs in a semi-circle was very successful.

12 fabricate (invent, make up something false)
   manufacture (make, produce in a factory)

    (a) To avoid suspicion, he decided to _____ a completely false story.
    (b) This is the factory where they _____ the new sports-car.
    (c) Any attempt to _____ evidence will be dealt with most severely by the courts.
    (d) Plans are in progress to _____ electrical appliances here, which will create much-needed jobs.

13 chauffeur (uniformed car-driver employed to drive others)
   driver (person who drives a car, lorry, bus etc.)

    (a) The police stopped every vehicle on the motorway and asked the _____ to show his or her licence.
    (b) She had her own Rolls Royce and her own _____ to drive her wherever she wanted to go.
    (c) He works as a _____, driving ministers and civil servants from place to place.
    (d) Any _____ about to stop, slow down or turn should clearly indicate his or her intentions to following vehicles.

14 assist (help)
   attend (be present at)

    (a) We hope a large number of people will _____ the conference next week.
    (b) The police called for members of the public to _____ in the investigation.
    (c) Due to a previous engagement, the Foreign Minister will be unable to _____ the meeting. A deputy will go instead.
    (d) Lifeboats were sent out to _____ the ship in difficulties.

15 pass (be successful in test, exam)
   take (attempt test, exam)

    (a) If I _____ the exam, I'll celebrate by giving a party.
    (b) I hope you're successful in the exam. When do you _____ it?
    (c) I _____ my driving test tomorrow. I hope I _____ it.

16 remark (say, make a comment)
   notice (happen to see)

    (a) He enjoyed his stay with us, but he did _____ that he hadn't slept well.
    (b) I thought I saw a strange-looking man outside the house. Did you _____ him?
    (c) I was in such a hurry that I didn't _____ what the weather was like.
    (d) I have often heard tourists _____ favourably on the number of parks in the city.

17 **souvenir** (something bought or taken home as a reminder of a visit, occasion etc.)
    memory (something remembered, ability to remember)

   (a) I bought a model policeman as a _____ of my visit to London.
   (b) Playing football with friends is perhaps my happiest childhood _____.
   (c) I still have an old Spanish railway timetable that I kept as a _____.
   (d) My _____ isn't so good as I get old.

18 **stamp** (postage-stamp, official mark on document etc.)
    print (picture made from engraved block)

   (a) What value _____ do I need for this letter, please?
   (b) Most of his work was oil-paintings and water-colours but he also produced the occasional _____.
   (c) I bought a beautiful _____ by Hokusai, the Japanese artist.
   (d) At the border, the official put a _____ in my passport showing the date and place.

19 **reunion** (gathering of old friends, colleagues after separation)
    meeting (gathering of people for social or formal discussion)

   (a) We have a _____ at the office every Friday to talk about plans and problems.
   (b) I haven't seen my old school friends for 15 years. It's time someone organized a _____.
   (c) They're having a _____ to discuss plans for a big _____ of soldiers who fought in the Battle of Alamein.

20 **sympathetic** (showing sympathy or understanding, willing to listen to others' problems)
    nice (pleasant)

   (a) She was a very _____ little girl. Everyone liked her.
   (b) He's usually rather impatient and unfriendly, but I must say he was very _____ when I told him about my family problems.
   (c) It was a _____ party. I enjoyed it.
   (d) The police were very _____ to my complaint about the noise but said they could do nothing about it.

21 **corps** [kɔː] (special military or diplomatic etc. group of people)
    corpse [kɔːps] (dead body)

   (a) The _____ was examined by a pathologist to determine the cause of death.
   (b) Members of the Diplomatic _____ have a special legal status when they are abroad.
   (c) There is to be a reorganization of the Royal Army Medical _____.
   (d) When the king died, his _____ was wrapped in gold robes and laid in a stone coffin.

22 **voyage** (journey by sea)
    journey (travelling from one place to another)

   (a) The liner *Titanic* struck an iceberg in the Atlantic and sank on her very first _____.
   (b) My _____ to work every morning takes about 40 minutes.
   (c) He went on a long _____ across Asia.
   (d) Before the opening of the Suez Canal, the _____ from Europe to India round Africa took several weeks.

23 **legend** (very old, possibly untrue, story)
    key (set of symbols and their meanings on a map etc.)

(a) The _____ of King Witold and his gold palace is a very amusing story but it has no foundation in fact.
(b) The _____ at the bottom of the map explains the various symbols used.
(c) The different parts of the diagram are numbered and you'll find the _____ to these on the opposite page.
(d) Some people regard the account as historical fact while others dismiss it as a _____.

24 **become** (grow, develop into)
    obtain (get possession of)

(a) Visitors to Britain from certain countries must _____ a visa.
(b) His only ambition was to _____ rich.
(c) As the electric current passes through it, it will _____ hot.
(d) You can _____ the necessary information from any post office.

25 **on the contrary** (introduces contradiction, opposite)
    on the other hand (introduces counter-argument)

(a) Good Lord, I'm not rich! _____, I'm constantly in debt.
(b) She's very intelligent, but _____ she's apt to be impatient.
(c) Yes, it's a very cosmopolitan city. _____, it's very expensive.
(d) I don't think he'll pass the exam. _____, I think he'll almost certainly fail.

26 **critic** (reviewer, person who writes newspaper article on new book, film etc.)
    review (article written by critic)

(a) Have you read the *Daily Express* _____ of that new Spanish film?
(b) She was the book-_____ of a literary magazine.
(c) One _____ wrote a very bad _____ of my play. The others liked it.

IDIOM

Alliterative Expressions

1 'Alliteration' is the repeated use of the same letter or sound, usually the first letter of successive words. It is often used in poetic language ('borne on the swollen, swaying, swishing seas'), publicity ('Buy Brown's Best British Biscuits') and newspaper headlines ('Fighting Football Fans Face Fines'). It is also found in the following common colloquial expressions. Put each one in its correct place in the sentences below.

ship-shape	**rat race**	**wishy-washy**
mish-mash	**chit-chat**	**brickbats**

(a) Tired of the ceaseless pressure of the competitive business world, he decided to leave the _____ and take over a small newsagent's shop in the country.

(b) A politician must be strong enough to withstand the _____ which are constantly directed at him by the media.

(c) He's a serious, rather cold man. He likes to get to the point straightaway in conversation and not waste time in idle _____.

(d) I like to see everything neat and tidy, everything in its place. I like to keep everything _____.

(e) Michael Wilson's latest play is a confusing mixture. It is neither a comedy, a serious work nor a musical, but a _____ of all three.

(f) A company's annual report must be clearly written and contain only the necessary facts. A report which is vague and _____ is useless and makes a bad impression.

2 Instructions as above.

zigzag	**sing-song**	**dilly-dally**
flip-flops	**sob-story**	**creepy-crawly**

(a) Go and get some biscuits from the shop and come straight back. Don't _____ on the way.

(b) It's too steep to climb straight up the side of the hill. Most people _____ to make it easier.

(c) He tried to get money from me by telling a _____ about losing his job and being ill, but I didn't believe him.

(d) If little Louise sees a beetle or a spider, she screams, 'There's a _____!'.

(e) To keep our spirits up on the long journey we had a _____.

(f) _____ are cheap, open sandals, each consisting of a rubber sole and a strap between the toes.

3 Instructions as above.

tittle-tattle	**hot-head**	**riff-raff**
shilly-shally	**tell-tale**	**topsy-turvy**

(a) You must make up your mind about the job quickly. If you _____ any longer, they'll withdraw the offer.

(b) He's a very calm, moderate person, but his brother is a _____ who is liable to get very upset and even violent over political matters.

(c) Oh, I don't believe those stories they tell about him. They're just _____.

(d) 'The club I belong to is very exclusive,' he said snobbishly, 'They only accept upper-class people, not ordinary, vulgar _____.'
(e) He denied any involvement in the murder, but police found _____ traces of blood on his clothing.
(f) In the morning he found the whole office _____ and realized it had been burgled.

Animals

1 Put each of the following phrases in its correct place in the sentences below.

crocodile tears	**dog-collar**	**bookworm**	**dark horse**
zebra crossing	**wolf-whistles**	**wild-goose**	
stag party	**puppy fat**	**chase**	

(a) He's always reading. He'll read anything. He's a real _____.
(b) He's a very informal priest. He rarely wears a _____.
(c) Little Johnnie's parents were worried that he was very big, but the doctor told them not to worry as it was only _____.
(d) He expressed his sympathy but I don't think he's really sorry. It was just _____.
(e) Some girls appreciate _____ but others are embarrassed by them.
(f) The safest place to cross the road is at the _____.
(g) 'Sorry I can't invite you, Mary,' said Peter, 'but it's a _____.'
(h) Jim is the favourite to win the race, but I think Alan is a _____ who could win and surprise everyone.
(i) I went all over the place trying to get what I wanted but I had no success at all. It was a _____.

2 Put each of the following phrases in its correct place in the sentences below.

fly on the wall	**dog-eared**	**frog in my**	**donkey's years**
cat's eyes	**bird's-eye view**	**throat**	**guinea pig**
pigeon-holes			**parrot-fashion**

(a) After a book has been used a lot, it tends to get a bit _____.
(b) I'd love to be a _____ when the American and Russian leaders meet for a private talk.
(c) From that mountain you'll get a _____ of the town and lake.
(d) Harry and I are old friends. We've known each other for _____.
(e) In the old days children learnt their lessons _____, scarcely knowing what they were saying.
(f) Down the middle of the road, reflecting the cars' headlights, are the _____.
(g) I was once a _____ in a medical experiment to test a new drug.
(h) Can I have a glass of water? I've got a _____.
(i) In offices and hotels, letters are often placed in little, open-ended compartments called _____ labelled with the letters of the alphabet.

3 Use each of the following animals as a verb by putting it in a suitable form in its correct space in the sentences below.

fox	**monkey**	**worm**	**hound**
dog	**ram**	**duck**	**badger**

(a) The thief in the stolen car refused to stop so the police were forced to _____ it with their own car.

(b) This machine is complicated and dangerous so don't _____ about with it.
(c) The children _____ their father to buy them a dog until he finally gave in and did so.
(d) He complained that because of his political beliefs he had been _____ by the press.
(e) To avoid being seen he _____ down behind the hedge.
(f) He tried to avoid telling me but after half an hour I managed to _____ the truth out of him.
(g) He managed to _____ his pursuers by changing cars three times and then escaping in disguise.
(h) All through her life she was _____ by misfortune.

Body

1   Parts of the body appear in some colloquial idiomatic adjectives describing various human states and characteristics, e.g. 'heavy-hearted' means 'sad'. For each adjective on the left below find the word or phrase on the right which has the same meaning.

(a) stout-hearted   generous
(b) tight-fisted   brave, resolute
(c) open-handed   dishonest, liable to steal
(d) hard-headed   conceited, self-important
(e) big-headed   hypocritical
(f) weak-kneed   silent, unwilling to speak
(g) light-fingered   mean, not generous
(h) tight-lipped   insensitive to criticism
(i) two-faced   businesslike, unemotional
(j) starry-eyed   cowardly, nervous
(k) thick-skinned   over-romantic

2   The following parts of the body are used as verbs in the sentences below. Put each one in its correct place.

shin	finger	mouth	head
back	elbow	thumb	head
foot	shoulder		

(a) I think we'd better _____ for the station. Our train leaves in half an hour.
(b) It's your fault! Don't leave me to _____ all the blame!
(c) There was a crowd of people there. I had to _____ my way through.
(d) They decided to _____ their way round Europe. They're experienced hitch-hikers.
(e) If customers _____ a book a lot, it gets dirty.
(f) I'm having my house painted. It's very expensive. I don't know how I'm going to _____ the bill.
(g) Bob couldn't hear me because of the noise so I had to _____ what I wanted to say.
(h) He's very fit and strong. Watch him _____ up that tree like a monkey.
(i) It has been announced that the Foreign Minister will _____ a delegation to visit China next month.
(j) A large manufacturing firm has offered to _____ the Himalayan Expedition.

55

Collocations

Certain common adjectives are sometimes emphasized, especially in colloquial language, with the addition of another adjective or noun in front of them, e.g. 'The water was icy cold.' 'The road was dead straight'. 'Icy' and 'dead' in these sentences mean 'extremely' or 'absolutely'.

1 Put each word from the following list in its correct space in the sentences below.

wide	**dog**	**pitch**	**brand**
stone	**dirt**	**stark**	**bone**

(a) I wouldn't employ him. He's _____ idle.
(b) It's an amazing price, _____ cheap!
(c) I was _____ tired after such a hard day's work.
(d) He couldn't hear a thing. He was _____ deaf.
(e) It's not second-hand. It's _____ new.
(f) This room's freezing and the window's _____ open!
(g) Here's a photo of him at three months, _____ naked.
(h) It was _____ dark. I couldn't see a thing.

2 Instructions as above.

fast	**bone**	**razor**	**blind**
wide	**crystal**	**paper**	**flat**

(a) She had a _____ sharp mind.
(b) She went to bed at seven and she was _____ asleep by ten past.
(c) The sea near those rocks is _____ clear.
(d) There's been no rain for months and the land is _____ dry.
(e) Sorry, I can't lend you anything. I'm _____ broke.
(f) He was _____ drunk. He couldn't even walk properly.
(g) The neighbours hear everything we say. The walls are _____ thin.
(h) It was 2 a.m. but I was still _____ awake.

3 Certain nouns are often preceded, in the same way as the adjectives above, by adjectives (or sometimes by nouns used as adjectives) to emphasize their completeness and convey the meaning of 'extreme' or 'total'. Put each word from the following list in its correct place in the sentences below.

thin	**all-out**	**dire**	**blank**
blind	**bitter**	**rock**	**broad**

(a) We'll never give up the struggle. We'll fight to the _____ end.
(b) He was never seen again. He just seemed to disappear into _____ air.
(c) Those starving people are in _____ need of food.
(d) I had last heard of her in Australia 20 years before. When she walked in, I looked at her in _____ amazement.
(e) Crime is very prevalent there. People are robbed in the street in _____ daylight.
(f) The fighting is escalating rapidly. Soon it will be _____ war.
(g) Prices have been falling rapidly. When they reach _____-bottom, I'll buy.
(h) His followers' attitude to him was nothing short of _____ devotion.

Colour

1 Put each of the following phrases in its correct place in the sentences below.

out of the blue	**to catch someone red-handed**	**in the red**
a black sheep	**once in a blue moon**	**red tape**
a Black Maria	**to have green fingers**	
green with envy	**in black and white**	

(a) The offer of a job sounded very good on the phone but I shan't believe it till I have it _____.

(b) I must remind you that this is a non-smoking office. I suspect that some of you have been smoking. If I happen _____, I'm afraid it will mean dismissal.

(c) The prisoners were taken from the court to the prison in _____.

(d) To import firearms into Britain you'll have to fill in a lot of forms. There's a lot of _____.

(e) If you want to be a successful gardener, of course you've got _____.

(f) The rest of the family were respectable, honest people but he was always in trouble. I'm afraid he was _____.

(g) When I saw him in a new sports car, I was _____.

(h) Tourists often go to the British Museum but most Londoners only go _____.

(i) The firm is _____. It owes a lot of money.

(j) I had lost touch with Jack, and then one night he arrived at my flat right _____. What a surprise!

2 Instructions as above.

to give the green light to	**a red-letter day**	**to see red**
rose-coloured spectacles	**a red herring**	**a blackleg**
a white-collar job	**a green belt**	
a white elephant	**a white lie**	

(a) Bill carried on working when his fellow-workers went on strike. He was very unpopular and they called him _____.

(b) He said he didn't want to have _____ and sit in an office all day.

(c) All round the city there is _____ of open country where building is restricted.

(d) She loves animals and tends _____ when she sees one being badly treated.

(e) He told _____ to avoid hurting his wife's feelings.

(f) That horrible painting Uncle Jack gave us is _____, I'm afraid. What can we do with it?

(g) Be realistic. You can't go through life looking at the world through _____.

(h) That day was a memorable one for me. It was _____. I'll never forget it.

(i) In class pupils sometimes introduce _____ to distract the teacher from his subject.

(j) The government has finally decided _____ the building of a tunnel at that point. Work will begin next year.

'Do' and 'Make'

1 Choose the correct word, 'do' or 'make', for each space in the sentences below.

(a) Storms can _____ a lot of damage.
(b) I must _____ some shopping. First I'll _____ a list of things I need.
(c) He moved along the seat to _____ room for her to sit down.
(d) I have a complaint to _____. Can I see the manager?
(e) I must _____ a phone-call. I have to _____ an appointment with my hairdresser.
(f) Are you hungry? Shall I _____ you a sandwich?
(g) I'll _____ my best to _____ all the necessary arrangements in time.
(h) Let's _____ some plans for next week-end.
(i) _____ Exercise 7 and try not to _____ any mistakes.
(j) A week's holiday will _____ wonders for your health.

2 Instructions as above.

(a) The dogs _____ a lot of noise but they won't _____ you any harm.
(b) I'll _____ you an offer for your car. What about £4,000?
(c) I'm afraid I have a confession to _____. I've lost your book.
(d) I _____ a part-time job every evening just to _____ a little extra money.
(e) I'm busy. I have a lot of work to _____.
(f) If you want to _____ more progress, you must _____ more effort.
(g) I have to _____ a decision quickly.
(h) I don't like to _____ excuses, but I was too busy to _____ my homework last night.
(i) Can you _____ me a favour and lend me £10?
(j) They always _____ me very welcome when I visit them.

3 Instructions as above.

(a) How were they able to _____ their escape? And they didn't _____ a sound!
(b) This photo doesn't really _____ her justice. She's much more attractive than this.
(c) _____ sure you lock the door when you leave.
(d) We _____ a lot of business with that firm.
(e) These are the laboratories where we _____ our research and hope, of course, to _____ important discoveries.
(f) He only wants to _____ friends. Don't _____ fun of him.
(g) A holiday would _____ you a lot of good. I'll _____ enquiries about hotels and trains.
(h) I would like to _____ a suggestion.
(i) There are signs that the two countries finally want to _____ peace.
(j) I've got so much housework to _____.

Fictional Characters in Everyday Language

1 The following are names of characters in popular British and American fiction. They are so well-known by all British people (even those who have never read or even heard of the original work) that they are often used in ordinary conversation. Put each one in its correct place in the sentences below.

Robin Hood	**Sherlock Holmes**	**Man Friday**
James Bond	**Robinson Crusoe**	**Superman**
Peter Pan	**Billy Bunter**	**Scrooge**

(a) During the war he was sent on dangerous secret missions abroad. Very exciting! He was a sort of _____.

(b) I think Alan should go on a diet and get more exercise. He's beginning to look like _____.

(c) He still has very youthful enthusiasms, and he's as slim and fit as he was 20 years ago. He's a _____.

(d) There are times when most of us would like to escape from all the pressures of city life and live a more simple, basic kind of _____ existence.

(e) Come on! I've never met anyone so reluctant to spend money, you _____!

(f) He's not very practical. What he needs is someone to look after him and do everything for him. He needs a _____.

(g) The firm is doing very badly and facing bankruptcy. I don't think it can survive. We don't just want a new director. We want a _____.

(h) Well, yes, he was a criminal and he stole a lot of money, but he helped a lot of people with it. He was a bit of a _____.

(i) How on earth did you guess his nationality, occupation and all those other things about him just from his appearance? You're a proper _____.

2 Instructions as above.

Walter Mitty	**Jekyll and Hyde**	**Little Lord Fauntleroy**
Big Brother	**Rip Van Winkle**	**Old Uncle Tom Cobbleigh and all**
Tarzan	**Cinderella**	

(a) He's a strange chap. Usually he's very pleasant and reasonable, but there are times when he gets very bad-tempered and almost violent. He's got a _____ personality.

(b) Joe was at the party, and the Smiths, and Mary and Mr Jackson, and Steve, and – well, _____.

(c) I don't like this new government proposal to put details of everyone's private life on computers. I can see it will mean greater efficiency and all that, but, well, it's a bit like _____, isn't it?

(d) I think the neighbours' kids should be allowed a bit of freedom to wear what they like and get dirty having fun, not made to look like _____.

(e) She's really exploited by her family. They make her do everything for them, cook, clean. . . She's a sort of _____.

(f) He's a body-builder and weight-lifter. Have you seen him in a swim-suit? He looks like _____.

(g) He sounds very impressive when he talks about his adventures and achievements, but it's all fantasy. He's a _____ character.

(h) Come on, _____, wake up! It's nearly lunch-time.

Food

1 Put each of the following colloquial words or phrases in its correct place in the sentences below.

the salt of the earth	**cup of tea**	**peanuts**
a butter-fingers	**a vegetable**	**the cream**
a piece of cake	**full of beans**	**in a jam**
money for jam	**nuts**	**sour grapes**

(a) Throw it to me! Oh, I've dropped it! I am _____.
(b) I said I'd pay him today, but my money's in the bank and it's just closed. Now I'm _____.
(c) That's a high salary for an easy job. It's _____.
(d) He never wants to do anything interesting. He just sits around all day. He's a bit of _____.
(e) To me £1,000 is a lot of money, but to a millionaire it's _____.
(f) That firm only employs the very best graduates. They only take _____.
(g) I think people who help the old, sick and homeless are _____.
(h) He's a bit tired and lifeless now, but after a nap he'll be _____.
(i) She now says she didn't really want the job that she failed to get, but I think it's just _____.
(j) That's a crazy idea of hers. She must be _____.
(k) She likes literature and classical music. Discothèques are not her _____.
(l) The exam was very easy. It was _____.

2 Complete the colloquial similies below with the correct items from the following list.

mustard	**cucumber**	**hot cakes**	**water**
beetroot	**toast**	**chalk and**	**jelly**
sardines	**pancake**	**cheese**	

(a) He never panics in a difficult situation. He stays as cool as a _____.
(b) She was very embarrassed. She went as red as a _____.
(c) No, we aren't cold. Your flat's very warm. We're as warm as _____.
(d) There are no hills or slopes for miles around. It's as flat as a _____.
(e) Some students are not very interested in the subject. Others are as keen as _____.
(f) John and his brother are as different as _____.
(g) That singer's new record is in great demand. It's selling like _____.
(h) In the rush-hour buses, people are packed like _____.
(i) I was terrified. I was shaking like a _____.
(j) She's very extravagant. She spends money like _____.

'Hand'

1 Put each of the following phrases in its correct place in the sentences below.

cap in hand   **to hand**   **offhand**
out of hand   **hand-to-mouth**   **underhand**

(a) I'm afraid I don't know her address _____. I'll tell you tomorrow after I've looked it up.
(b) He wouldn't have minded so much if they had told him to his face that they wanted to dismiss him. It was the _____ way in which they did it that upset him.
(c) I'd rather borrow from the bank at high interest than go _____ to my father.
(d) The situation is now _____. The authorities admit that they cannot control the rioting and crime.
(e) He makes just enough money to provide for his basic daily needs. It's a wretched, _____existence.
(f) She always has pencil and paper _____ in case she suddenly sees an interesting person or place she wants to sketch.

2 Instructions as above.

high-handed   **short-handed**   **in good hands**
offhand   **empty-handed**   **single-handed**

(a) His manner was deceptively casual and _____. In fact he was a very serious, decisive person.
(b) We left the car with my brother-in-law. He's very careful and reliable so we knew it was _____.
(c) The shops were shut so I couldn't buy her a present. I felt bad arriving _____.
(d) I think you were rather _____ in dismissing him without consulting me or giving him a chance to explain.
(e) Three people were off sick at the office today so we were very _____.
(f) She was the first woman to sail the Atlantic _____. Her only problem was loneliness.

3 Instructions as above.

to wash his hands of   **to have a hand in**
to have the upper hand   **to keep his hand in**
to give him a free hand   **to win hands down**

(a) I think we ought _____ and let him carry out the scheme as he thinks best without any interference from us.
(b) He gave up playing the piano professionally years ago but he still likes _____ by playing a little from time to time.
(c) He wants nothing more to do with the idea. He just wants _____ the whole thing.
(d) The guerrillas are reported _____. The government forces are very much on the defensive.
(e) My older brother always beat me easily at tennis. He always used _____.
(f) He is thought _____ a gold-smuggling operation now going on but the police can't prove it.

Letter-Words and Phrases

1 The first part of each of the following words consists of a single letter. What do the words mean? Put each word in its correct place in the sentences below.

A-bomb	**T-shirt**	**U-turn**	**V-neck**
L-plates	**T-junction**	**V-formation**	**X-ray**
S-bend			

(a) Drive straight on and then turn left at the _____.
(b) The invention and use of the _____ introduced a terrible new era of modern warfare.
(c) On holiday I just wear a _____, shorts and sandals.
(d) Drive carefully here. There's a dangerous _____ just ahead.
(e) The government has done a complete _____ in its trade policy. It now wants to increase imports instead of reducing them.
(f) Before you have a full driving licence in Britain, you have to have _____ on your car and be accompanied by a qualified driver.
(g) The doctors could tell from the _____ that his leg was broken.
(h) The president's car was preceded by nine police motor-cyclists in a _____.
(i) I bought a lambswool _____ pullover.

2 What do the italicized phrases in the following sentences mean?

(a) He's visiting his girl-friend's parents for the first time and wants to make a good impression. He'll *have to watch his p's and q's.*
(b) Where's Grafton Street? Have you got *an A to Z?*
(c) She's a snob. She looks down on people who *drop their h's.*
(d) I'm not against modern educational methods, but I think that the basis of learning for children should still be *the three R's.*

Names

1 Some common names appear in idiomatic expressions. Put each of the following items in its correct place in the sentences below.

peeping Tom	**smart Alec**	**Jack of all trades**
doubting Thomas	**bobby**	**Tom, Dick or Harry**

(a) A British policeman is sometimes called a '_____'. The name comes from Sir Robert Peel, the founder of the first London police force.
(b) It is often said of someone who can do many different things that he is a _____.
(c) Someone who spies on other people, especially by looking through their windows, is called a _____.
(d) Oh, don't take any notice of him. He thinks he knows everything. He's just a _____.
(e) He's a real snob. He's only interested in people who are rich or famous. He won't talk to any _____.
(f) When the Wright brothers invented the first aeroplane which actually flew, there was many a _____ who said that air-travel would never be commercially successful.

2 Instructions as above.

keeping up with the Joneses
robbing Peter to pay Paul
I don't know him from Adam
before you could say Jack Robinson

(a) No, I'm sure I've never met him. He's a complete stranger. Really, _____.

(b) The couple next door are very conscious of their social position. They've got a new car, a modern kitchen, trendy new clothes. They don't really need them. They're just _____.

(c) One man insulted another and suddenly, _____, they were involved in a violent fight.

(d) It's ridiculous to borrow from your uncle to settle your debt to your cousin. That's just _____.

Numbers

1 Put each of the following expressions in its correct place in the sentences below.

one-armed bandit
one-track mind
one-man band

two-edged compliment
three-cornered contest
four-letter word
nine-day wonder

(a) It seems a big event now and everyone's talking about it, but I think people will have forgotten about it soon. It's just a _____.

(b) She said I looked very good for my age. That was rather a _____, wasn't it?

(c) A gambling machine where you put a coin in and pull a lever at the side is sometimes called a _____.

(d) The only thing he thinks about is money. He's got a _____.

(e) Television viewers protested at the use of a _____ in a programme last night. They said they were disgusted and shocked.

(f) Although he has occasional help, the firm is really a _____.

(g) The candidates for the presidency are Gonzalez, Martinez and Silva. It's a _____.

2 Instructions as above.

to have second thoughts
in her seventh heaven
to play second fiddle
at the eleventh hour

on first name terms
the third degree
sixth sense
third-rate

(a) The security forces denied accusations that they had used _____ on prisoners to make them confess.

(b) He was a brilliant journalist who seemed to have a _____ which told him when and where something important was going to happen.

(c) It's a very friendly company to work in. Everyone's _____.

(d) She was _____ when she actually met her favourite film-star. She'll never forget it.

(e) He likes to be his own boss. He'll never agree _____ to anyone else.

(f) No, it wasn't a very good film. In fact it was pretty _____.
(g) At first she liked him, but now she's beginning _____.
(h) Our financial problems were so great that we thought we'd have to sell our house, but _____ my father-in-law lent us some money.

Pairs

1 Put each of the following colloquial 'pair-phrases' in its correct place in the sentences below.

cloak and dagger	**length and breadth**	**hard and fast**
chop and change	**song and dance**	**by and large**
pins and needles	**tooth and nail**	
prim and proper	**collar and tie**	

(a) Don't dress casually tonight. It's going to be a _____ occasion.
(b) She's very strict in moral matters and rather a snob. She's very

_____.

(c) I agree that the shop treated you very badly. But just write a polite letter of complaint. It's not worth making a _____ about it.
(d) Of course a few pupils were lazy, but _____ the children were interested and hard-working.
(e) If you take a decision, you must stick to it. You can't _____ all the time.
(f) When the old man died, his greedy relatives fought _____ over his will.
(g) We don't regard our entry requirements as _____ rules. We are prepared to be flexible.
(h) He knows Britain very well. He's travelled the _____ of the country.
(i) I like exciting novels about spies and conspiracies. I love that _____ stuff.
(j) If you've been sitting in one position for a long time without moving, you sometimes get _____.

2 Instructions as above.

safe and sound	**ups and downs**	**odds and ends**	**up and about**
sick and tired	**to and fro**	**ins and outs**	**down and out**
pros and cons	**spick and span**		

(a) I'm _____ of his continual bad behaviour.
(b) She's very house-proud. Her kitchen is always _____.
(c) I just keep various _____ in that drawer, nothing special.
(d) Like everyone else, she has her _____ of course, but on the whole she's quite satisfied with life.
(e) He lost everything, family, job, money, home. . . Now he's _____ and sleeping in the park.
(f) You should consider the _____ carefully before you make a decision.
(g) She's ill in bed, but she'll be _____ in a couple of days.
(h) The parents were beginning to worry but finally the children arrived home _____.
(i) This ferry-boat operates between England and France. It just goes _____ all the time.
(j) He's the right man for the job. He's experienced. He knows the _____ of the business.

Phrasal Verbs

1 Put each of the following phrasal verbs in its correct place in the sentences below.

get down	**bring up**	**take down**	**call off**
try out	**bring up**	**put up**	**see off**

(a) Don't worry about the journey to the airport. I'm coming to _____ you _____.

(b) The other car didn't stop after the accident but luckily I was able to _____ its number.

(c) The car's in quite good condition but you can _____ it _____ before you make any decision to buy.

(d) Would you like to _____ any other matters before the meeting closes?

(e) Stop worrying about it. Don't let this failure _____ you _____.

(f) I'm afraid we'll have to _____ the meeting _____. Alice and John can't come.

(g) Her parents died when she was eight and her uncle decided to _____ her _____ himself.

(h) I've got a spare room, so I can _____ you _____ if you're ever here again.

2 Instructions as above.

run down	**bear out**	**make up**	**let down**
rule out	**put forward**	**put off**	**leave out**

(a) I'm depending on you to pay me back the money on Monday. Please don't _____ me _____.

(b) To cover his absence he decided to _____ a completely false story about being involved in a car accident.

(c) If you think I'm wrong, check in the encyclopaedia. I'm sure it will _____ me _____.

(d) Because of pressure of work, he had to _____ his summer holiday until October.

(e) We want to give younger players a chance in the team. That's why we've decided to _____ you _____ of next Saturday's match.

(f) They're very two-faced. They're very nice to her when she's there, but they _____ her _____ behind her back.

(g) I'd like to _____ a proposal. I suggest we start production in May.

(h) The government intend to take very serious measures against this interference in their country's affairs. They do not _____ the possibility of military action.

3 Instructions as above.

give away	**do up**	**turn away**	**put up**
look up	**put off**	**pull down**	**turn out**

(a) The authorities intend to _____ these old buildings and _____ a modern office block in their place.

(b) They'll never believe you're American. Your British accent will _____ you _____ immediately.

(c) If you persist in refusing to pay the rent for this flat, we shall have no option but to _____ you _____.

(d) When I was in New York, I was able to _____ several old friends I hadn't seen for years.
(e) We're very sorry to have to _____ you _____, but I'm afraid the hotel is fully booked.
(f) The flat hasn't been very well looked after, but I think that after I _____ it _____ it'll look very nice.
(g) The old-fashioned appearance of the hotel might _____ some people, but in fact it's really very modern and comfortable inside.

4 Instructions as above.

take to	**stand for**	**get over**	**account for**
come into	**get round**	**run into**	**take after**

(a) The initials V.I.P. _____ Very Important Person.
(b) Scientists are mystified by the sudden increase in the world's temperature. They are quite unable to _____ it.
(c) I don't think he'll ever completely _____ his wife's death. He'll always miss her.
(d) John works in that office. I quite often _____ him in the streets round here.
(e) I can't think of a way to _____ the problem.
(f) She has a very pleasant manner. I'm sure the children will _____ her at once.
(g) He expects to _____ a lot of money in his grandfather's will.
(h) My father and I have the same character. I _____ him much more than my mother.

5 Instructions as above.

make up for	**be up to**	**look down on**	**catch up with**
put up with	**be up to**	**do away with**	**go back on**

(a) If they _____ their promise, I'll never trust them again.
(b) You must make your suggestion to the director. Then it'll _____ him to decide.
(c) He missed a month's school through illness, so now he'll have to work hard to _____ the other pupils.
(d) I don't think I can _____ this noise any longer. I'm going mad.
(e) I'm sorry we had to cancel the party, but to _____ it let's all go to the cinema.
(f) The growing use of credit cards may ultimately _____ the use of cash altogether.
(g) There are some strange noises coming from Jane's room. What on earth can she _____?
(h) I'm afraid they're very snobbish. They _____ their poorer relations.

6 Instructions as above.

break up	**go off**	**come out**	**break out**
turn in	**look up**	**turn up**	**fall through**

(a) It's past midnight and I'm tired. I think I'll _____.
(b) I waited nearly an hour for them, but they didn't _____.
(c) After all the trouble you've taken, I hope your plans don't _____.
(d) There is a very real fear that war may _____ soon.
(e) We've had some hard times recently, but I think things are beginning to _____.

(f) The emergency services thought that the bomb might _____ at any moment.

(g) The schools _____ next week. It's almost holiday-time.

(h) Her new book is due to _____ next month. I wonder what the critics will think of it.

7 Instructions as above.

go down	**drop off**	**break down**	**come up**
fall out	**drop in**	**fall off**	**hold on**

(a) The number of tourists visiting Britain is at its peak in July and August and begins to _____ in September.

(b) The subject of higher salaries will probably _____ at the meeting.

(c) Don't get so nervous about your speech tonight. I'm sure it'll _____ very well.

(d) She's not a very strong person. I'm afraid she might _____ when she hears the news.

(e) They haven't spoken to each other since that argument about the taxi fare. How silly to _____ over such a trivial thing.

(f) I think we're going in the wrong direction. _____, I'll look at the map.

(g) I live at 32, Rutherford Street. _____ if you're in the district.

(h) The meeting was long and the room was hot. I was afraid I might _____.

Rhyming Expressions

1 A number of common colloquial expressions consist of rhyming parts. Put each of the following expressions in its correct place in the sentences below.

go-slow	**big-wigs**	**pell-mell**	**higgledy-**
nitty-gritty	**prime-time**	**humdrum**	**piggledy**
brain-drain			

(a) We've got some important visitors coming to see the factory tomorrow. They're government inspectors, Members of Parliament, officials from the Ministry and other _____.

(b) The programme is only of limited interest. I can't understand why it's shown on _____ television.

(c) The two world leaders met and after the usual greetings and formalities got down to the _____ of their talks.

(d) It wasn't exactly a strike. All the workers did as little as possible. It was a _____.

(e) After the robbery everything was in a mess, _____ all over the place.

(f) She'd like to find a more interesting, exciting job. She finds her present work very _____.

(g) It's been a terrible morning. I overslept, rushed out _____ to the bus-stop, missed the bus, had to get a taxi. . .

(h) The _____ of doctors, scientists and academics leaving this country is having a serious effect on our health service, industries and universities.

2 Instructions as above.

silly-billy	**hanky-panky**	**space-race**	**walkie-talkie**
mumbo-jumbo	**willy-nilly**	**fun-run**	**roly-poly**

(a) A policeman usually carries a _____ so that he can keep in touch with his police station.
(b) 5,000 people are taking part in a five-mile _____ on Sunday to raise money for charity.
(c) You've put on weight. You're getting quite _____.
(d) Oh, I am a _____. I've bought salt and I meant to buy sugar.
(e) The competition between the United States and the Soviet Union in the field of rockets and inter-planetary exploration is often called the _____.
(f) She did not believe in having a religious wedding and considered the church service to be just a lot of _____.
(g) In the army you don't have much choice where you go. You're sent where you're needed, _____.
(h) There have been accusations of illegalities, suspicious irregularities and other _____ during the elections. There's going to be an inquiry.

3 Instructions as above.

wine and dine	**moan and**	**meals-on-**	**wear and tear**
la-di-da	**groan**	**wheels**	**make or break**

(a) Old people who cannot cook for themselves easily are entitled to use the _____ service.
(b) This is Wayne Smith's last chance to show if he is good enough for the English football team. It's _____ day for him.
(c) She was very affected in her accent and manner. Most people thought she was very _____.
(d) After twelve years it's only natural that your furniture is showing signs of _____.
(e) Come to the best restaurant in town, where you can _____ in style.
(f) If you find so much to complain about in your job, either do something about it or resign. Don't just _____.

'Say' and 'Tell'

In addition to introducing speech, 'say' and 'tell' are also used in a number of idiomatic phrases. Use the correct word in a suitable form in the following sentences.

(a) Bobby is only three and can't _____ the time yet.
(b) I like the idea. There's a lot to be _____ for it.
(c) Of course, you can have your medical treatment done privately but, needless to _____, it'll be more expensive.
(d) Most people, _____ 85%, are against the government on this matter.
(e) I can't _____ the difference between butter and margarine.
(f) Look at that sunset! I _____! How marvellous.
(g) I think ordinary people should have a greater _____ in local government.

(h) He was punished for _____ lies.
(i) Britain is a member of the EEC, that is to _____, the European Economic Community.
(j) It goes without _____ that you're always welcome at my home.
(k) You can _____ the age of a horse by its teeth.
(l) She's very quiet and timid. She wouldn't _____ boo to a goose.
(m) If you want any help, I'm ready and willing. Just _____ the word.
(n) Though I _____ it myself, I'm pretty good at my job.
(o) You can _____ a man by the company he keeps.
(p) 'You look as tired and hot as I am. I think it's time to stop and have a drink.' 'You can _____ that again.'
(q) Whether the agreement between the two countries will last, only time will _____.

Status

Use the correct phrase from the following list to replace each of the phrases in italics in the sentences below.

The headmaster-to-be	The so-called headmaster
The late headmaster	The would-be headmaster
The present headmaster	The ex-headmaster
The headmaster present	The stop-gap headmaster
The actual headmaster	The sacked headmaster
The headmaster in question	

(a) *The man determined to be headmaster* made a speech.
(b) *The headmaster, who is now dead,* made a speech.
(c) *The headmaster who was at the occasion* made a speech.
(d) *The man who had previously been headmaster* made a speech.
(e) *The man who is now headmaster* made a speech.
(f) *The headmaster who was dismissed* made a speech.
(g) *The headmaster himself* made a speech.
(h) *The man who was temporarily acting as headmaster until someone was appointed permanently* made a speech.
(i) *The headmaster who is the subject of discussion* made a speech.
(j) *The man who was due to take up his appointment as headmaster* made a speech.
(k) *The headmaster, who I think is very bad at his job,* made a speech.

Time

1 Put each of the following phrases in its correct place in the sentences below.

at the time	for the time being	in time
at one time	at times	on time

(a) _____ the streets of London were lit by gas, but that was at least a hundred years ago.
(b) Soon after they met, they decided to get married. _____ it seemed an ideal match. Within a few years, however, their different personalities began to cause friction.

(c) She's quite happy in England on the whole, but of course she misses Brazil _____.

(d) We're painting our son's bedroom, so _____ he's sleeping in our room.

(e) The trains are very punctual. They always leave _____.

(f) When she heard her father was dying, she immediately went to the hospital and arrived just _____.

2 Instructions as above.

pressed for time	**in his time**	**at the same time**
behind the times	**before my time**	**in no time**

(a) My father's been to almost every country in the world _____.

(b) We must keep up to date. We can't compete successfully with other firms if we get _____ in our methods.

(c) He's looking forward to starting his new job, but _____ he's a bit nervous.

(d) I'm afraid I can't talk to you at the moment. I'm a bit _____.

(e) Someone called Wilkins used to be the head of this firm, but I never met him. It was _____.

(f) She's very bright and quick. She learnt to use a computer _____.

3 Instructions as above.

all in good time	**time after time**	**for old time's sake**
in the nick of time	**about time too**	**time on his hands**

(a) The firemen got the children out _____. Less than a minute later the building collapsed.

(b) You can have a bicycle, and I'll get you a camera. But not yet. _____.

(c) I met an old school-friend the other day. He was down on his luck and out of work. I doubt if he's really very efficient but I got him a job in my firm just _____.

(d) Ah, here you are! _____! I've been waiting an hour.

(e) Having been busy all his life, he finds it strange to have _____ now that he's retired. He doesn't know what to do with himself.

(f) I've warned them about it _____ but they never listen.

4 Instructions as above.

bide his time	**make time**	**keep up with**
take his time	**kill time**	**the times**

(a) He's old and he's not well. Don't hurry him. Let him _____.

(b) I don't like the new methods very much but I suppose we must _____.

(c) He wasn't due to meet Jill for another hour so he went for a walk in the park, just to _____.

(d) Well, I'm pretty busy, Mr Fraser, but I can always _____ to see an old customer.

(e) He wants to be President but he's waiting for the right moment. He's decided to _____ until circumstances are favourable.

IDENTIFICATION

Objects

In each of the following passages someone is referring to a well-known object. Identify each object and give at least five words which helped you to decide.

(a) The mudguards are a bit loose and quite a bit of wet comes up at me when it's raining and the gears don't work very well and there are a couple of spokes missing. And maybe I should replace the pedals. They're worn and my feet slipped off this morning and I had to hang onto the handlebars and pull up quickly. Luckily the brake-blocks were OK.

(b) It's quite posh-looking, made of calf, hand-sewn, with brass hinges. There are compartments inside the lid for various documents. It's 16" × 12" × 3" and it's got my initials in gold near the handle.

(c) I can easily find the volume knob to turn it up because it's on the far right at the bottom. And then there's the brightness control next to it and then the buttons for the different channels. The picture's good except for a bit of a flicker sometimes and there's interference when someone's using a vacuum-cleaner. Otherwise it's OK.

(d) The frontispiece is a photograph of Churchill. It's very much thumbed and coffee-stained, the binding is loose and the spine is so faded that you can scarcely read the title. God knows where the dust-jacket went. It was pretty tattered anyway.

(e) It's nothing special, not a grand, just an ordinary old upright. Needs tuning, as you'll hear. Open the lid and you'll see the keyboard. The pedals are a bit stiff. Sit down. Have a go.

(f) The face is a bit scratched and the strap is only plastic, with a cheap metal buckle. You wind it by turning the little knob. The case is stainless steel. It cost me about fifteen quid.

(g) There's not much foliage at the moment. It's deciduous. But it still looks lovely to me. I like the rough bark and the sturdy trunk. Just think, a hundred years ago it was just a sapling. I hope they don't plan to fell it.

(h) Take a look at this. Hold it. Touch the trigger. Spin the chamber. That's where you put the cartridges in. This is the safety-catch, but don't worry, it's not loaded. In fact I've got no ammunition. How would you like to find yourself staring into the muzzle of a thing like this?

(i) Let me unfold it. Here's the scale at the bottom, and the key to the various symbols is in the corner. The relief is shown by contour-lines. I love these things. I should have been a cartographer.

Newspaper Parts

Below are 18 typical extracts from different parts of a newspaper. Identify each one with one of the following words or phrases.

obituary	**football report**	**television preview**
headline	**horoscope**	**crossword clues**
gossip column	**auction report**	**weather forecast**
recipe	**new car report**	**readers' advice column**
caption	**court circular**	**parliamentary report**
editorial	**gardening tips**	**travel and holidays**

(a) Starting overcast with intermittent rain, followed by sunny spells. Max. temp. 21°C.

(b) The word is that Clinton Ross, 32, playboy son of US steel billionaire Dwight Ross, has left his girlfriend, actress Lee-Ann Van Post, 26, and is now in Europe.

(c) Prince Edward (left) enjoys a joke with actor Sam Cool (centre).

(d) PREMIER TO PROBE RIDDLE OF 'SPIES IN MINISTRY'

(e) He received a number of international literary awards, culminating in the Nobel Prize for Literature in 1986. He leaves a widow and two sons.

(f) Today is a good day to do business but a bad one for romance. Don't take members of the opposite sex too seriously today.

(g) Our front page today gives details of the government's new economic proposals. Our readers may think, as we do, that these measures are too little and too late. We say to the government, not for the first time, it is time. . .

(h) Mix two egg yolks with butter in a frying-pan over a low gas. Add sugar and then. . .

(i) A pair of silver George II candlesticks fetched £17,000. Bidding was slow for Victorian oil paintings but a landscape by Somers went for £55,000.

(j) Yesterday at 7 p.m. Her Majesty gave a dinner-party at Windsor Castle for members of the Spanish Royal Family. At noon today Her Majesty will receive the new Ambassador of the Republic of Venezuela at Buckingham Palace.

(k) Robson equalised with a header from five yards just before the half-time whistle.

(l) The cheapest bucket-shop air-return to Hong Kong is now about £480 and Hong Kong is a good base to visit Macao, China and Taiwan. The best season is. . .

(m) ACROSS 1 kind of tree (5), 2 child (3), 4 performed (5). . .

(n) Mr Richard Caulder (West Hull, Labour) asked if the Minister of Transport could inform MPs of train-fare concessions for pensioners. However, the Speaker declared that. . .

(o) Now is the time to plant roses. Put trees in at least 2' apart, and cover roots with 6" of soil.

(p) . . . but I don't know if I can ever forgive him. What can I do? Desperately Unhappy, London N.W. Dear Desperately Unhappy, I think you should see a marriage-guidance counsellor. . .

(q) A hard-hitting documentary series starts tonight at 10 p.m. Viewers might be shocked at scenes of. . .

(r) Road holding and fuel consumption are good but otherwise the performance lacks zip.

The Arts

The following are parts of newspaper reviews of visual and performing arts and literature. Identify the subject of each (film, novel etc.) and give at least six words which helped you to decide.

(a) The first movement is dominated by the strings with only occasional percussion participation. So many bows dancing in unison made this a visual as well as an aural delight and I abandoned my score to watch. In the second movement the wind section takes command, and with such vigour that the baton seems to struggle to keep up rather than the reverse. For once I did not envy the man on the rostrum, and was content with my seat in the stalls.

(b) His favourite medium is now oil, and the canvas which dominates this show, a still-life of bottles, is a masterpiece of representational skill (his early abstracts and collages were never good). His technique is superb. The brush-strokes are invisible, the bottles real. Every section of his palette is used. I shall never again think of bottles as colourless. Every hue of the spectrum is there.

(c) Her weaknesses are characterization and dialogue. Her strengths are plot and feeling for place. Her characters are two-dimensional, their words wooden, but the events are plausible and the places vividly depicted. The setting is now Mexico City, now Tokyo, now Johannesburg. The twist at the end defies prediction. For once the blurb on the back is true. It says, 'Unputdownable'.

(d) This new young choreographer has given us an exciting and unconventional piece. Called simply *Mixture*, it is indeed influenced by classical, folk, progressive and even tap and ballroom besides. The men are agile and athletic, the girls loose-limbed and supple. The leaps are high, the pirouettes prolonged. What more can you want? The night I went they received a standing ovation.

(e) First-night nerves are notorious, but I have never heard so many lines fluffed, so many cues missed. The prompter was busy last night and the director (and doubtless the backers) in tears. I do not expect this piece to have a long run, but critical reception and box-office success are often two very different things and, if it does survive, it will have been saved by a number of well-played supporting roles and a stunning set. But the final final curtain cannot, I think, be far off.

(f) His fashion and portrait work is mostly posed and static. His lens does not seek out the spontaneous gesture or unexpected expression. He uses filters and lighting expertly. Otherwise his images owe more to expertise in the darkroom than inspiration in the studio. The prints are sharp and clear, the close-ups remarkable for their detail.

(g) In Britain sub-titles are normally preferred, but this is dubbed. It is a low-budget work shot mainly on location in a Swiss village, with local people as extras, a director unknown in this country and a natural mountain setting which looks spectacular and cost nothing. The sensitive playing of the two leads, also unknown here, is brilliant. I predict awards for this one.

Occupations

In each of the following passages someone is talking about his or her occupation. Identify each occupation and give at least five words or phrases which helped you to decide.

(a) Most of my customers are very particular. They want wide lapels or narrow lapels, a single vent or a double vent or no vent at all, turn-ups or plain bottoms. Flared trousers are out nowadays, so are tapered. Everyone wants them straight. Some people are even fussy about the lining. Everyone wants to be trendy.

(b) When I start at 8.30, the baskets are already stacked, the trolleys are lined up near the door and the shelf-fillers have done their work. I make sure I've got a supply of carrier bags and enough change in the till and I'm ready to start.

(c) We get the latest weather briefing from the Met. chaps and then we board. We say hello to the cabin crew, do a complete cockpit check, then wait for instructions through the headphones to start taxi-ing out to the runway.

(d) I've got a busy morning here. I've got to prepare some beds for sowing by weeding and raking. I've got to take up a worn bit of lawn and lay some new turf and I've got to do some pruning. Then there's a lot needs doing in the greenhouse. . .

(e) Two discharges today, but five admissions and Mrs Crowther's got to go to theatre this afternoon. They have their mid-morning tea at eleven, then, since it's Tuesday, the specialist will be doing his round at half-past. And there are always relatives' phone-calls to deal with. Next week I'm on night-shift. Excuse me, I must go and change some dressings.

(f) I picked up a fare at the station today. I was in the rank. Smartly-dressed chap. Wanted St Michael's Church. 'Going to a wedding?' I said. 'Yes, and I'm late. Step on it,' he said. I did my best and as I dropped him off I said, 'Doesn't look as if they've started yet.' 'They can't,' he said, 'I'm the bridegroom.' And he didn't give me a tip!

(g) Of course my prime concern is the needs of my parishioners, but I'm also worried about the building itself. The pews at the front need replacing, the pulpit's got a crack in it and the bell-ringers tell me the belfry needs attention. We have a limited income. We're largely dependent on the collections, and our congregation is rather small, I'm afraid. And we do need a new altar-cloth. . .

(h) We're fully-dressed in our helmets and protective clothing by the time we arrive. Then we start unrolling the hoses and getting the ladders ready in case they're needed. The worst things are hoax alarms. You can never be sure till you get there whether a call is genuine or not. Some people think it's fun to dial 999. . .

(i) I flashed my torch at where they were supposed to go, but they went further down the aisle and along the wrong row. Luckily it was only during the credits or trailer or something, so they didn't disturb people too much. It's usually a pretty routine job, but last week the projectionist fell asleep just before he was supposed to change reels!

(j) When I'm covering a story, I always have to remember my deadline, which is 7 p.m., to catch the following day's first edition. It's a hectic job but I enjoy it, and I always dream of getting a scoop or ending up as editor one day. Who knows?

Occasions

Each of the following passages is part of a description of an occasion or event. Identify the subject of each description, giving at least six words which helped you to decide.

(a) A warning was given by an anonymous caller saying he represented a separatist movement. The area was evacuated and cordoned off, and attempts were made to defuse the device, but it detonated soon after midnight. Emergency services are now at the scene and are ensuring that no one is left in the building, trapped under the rubble.

(b) It was all very traditional. The big top, an enormous, striped, canvas thing, was pitched in a car-park and, inside, the wooden benches rose in tiers round the sawdust-filled ring. The high wire was fixed across the top and various bits of equipment were placed outside the ring ready for use, a trampoline, spring-boards and so on. When everyone had taken their seats, the band struck up and the master of ceremonies in his top hat and tails made his entrance.

(c) Spokesmen for both parties have announced at a news conference that the atmosphere has been frank and cordial and aides of the principal participants have spoken of a 'détente' but the rumour among the media is that hard words have been spoken. Although efforts have been made to portray the proceedings of the last few days as a routine, low-key occasion, it is widely thought that the aim has been to pave the way for a summit in the late autumn.

(d) At the gates there were crowds of pickets being held back by police. Anyone who went in had to run the gauntlet of jeers, cat-calls and shouts of 'scab, scab, scab'. Inside, the machines stood idle and the management held meetings to discuss whether to take a hard line, to submit the dispute to arbitration, to appease the work-force with an acceptable compromise or simply to cave in and meet all demands.

(e) The jurors filed in and took their places without a glance at the dock, where Smith stood passively. The opposing counsel, their work done, tidied their briefs, smoothed their gowns and put away their books. In the public gallery they talked in low tones. The ushers stood silently at their posts. Then the clerk of the court rose to his feet and cleared his throat. . .

(f) The procession moved down the main shopping street chanting slogans, each group behind its leaders, who carried banners and placards. There had been isolated scuffles but, on the whole, the stewards did their job well and onlookers were impressed by the orderliness of the occasion. When the marchers reached the square, they spread out in front of the platform, on either side of which loudspeakers were directed out towards the footsore crowds.

(g) Most polls have indicated that the LOP will get in by a landslide, but pollsters can blunder and there are those whose money is on the PDM by a narrow majority. In the meantime, door-to-door canvassing continues and campaigning proceeds fast and furious. This will go on until Tuesday, when the focus of attention will shift from platform to polling station and the actual balloting takes place. A large turn-out is expected.

DESCRIPTION

Diagrams

The exercises below give practice in comprehension of expressions which indicate position, shape and size. Draw accurately the diagrams described.

Example: From the mid-point of a vertical broken line, a dotted line extends horizontally to the right. This line is twice the length of the vertical line.

Answer:

(a) A capital 'E' is the wrong way round. Its middle horizontal extends (to the left) so that it is three times as long as each of the other horizontals.

(b) A square has a wavy line for its upper side. The top right-hand corner of the square is connected to the centre of the square with a straight diagonal line.

(c) A broken line runs horizontally across a circle connecting the centre of the circle and each side. In the centre of the lower half of the circle is a capital 'Y' upside-down.

(d) The basic shape is a rectangle with the vertical sides twice as long as the horizontals. A wavy diagonal line connects the top right-hand corner of the rectangle with the bottom left-hand corner. In the right angle of the lower triangle thus formed is a small capital 'A' upside-down. Above the top horizontal, near the left-hand end, is a capital 'S' the wrong way round. From the centre of the right-hand vertical line, a dotted horizontal line extends to the right, the same length as each of the other horizontals, linking with the mid-point of a third vertical line which stands parallel to the other two and of the same length. A straight broken line joins the top end of this vertical line with the bottom right-hand corner of the rectangle, making it parallel with the wavy line.

Write descriptions, like those above, of the following diagrams.

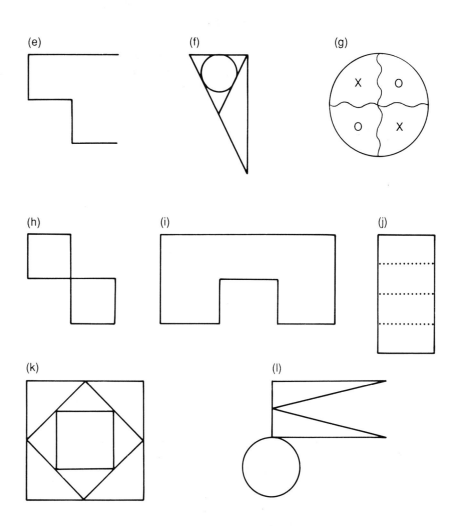

(e)

(f)

(g)

(h)

(i)

(j)

(k)

(l)

Plans

The exercises below give practice in comprehension of common expressions of position, shape and size. Draw accurately each plan described.

Example: My armchair faces the television set, which has a round vase on it in the middle and a small clock on the right of the vase. Immediately to the left of the armchair, as you sit in it, is an oval table with its greater length parallel to the arms of the chair.

Answer:

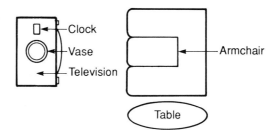

(a) My rectangular desk is about half as wide as it is long and I sit at the left-hand end of one of the longer sides on a chair with a curved back. The telephone is on my right and my business diary is in the corner furthest from me. My typewriter is in the middle of the left-hand half of the desk.

(b) The park is triangular in shape with the entrance in the middle of the longest side, facing the right-angle corner of the park. To the left as you go in, in the corner, is a round pond with four benches equally spaced round it. A straight path goes right, at an angle, from inside the entrance to a statue of Queen Victoria which stands in the middle of the side facing the pond. On either side of the statue a row of trees extends to the corners of the park.

(c) The postage stamp is square and has a vertical line from top to bottom a quarter of the way in from the right-hand side. Taking up most of the rectangle on the left is a picture of the head of President Kennedy, facing left, below which, in the bottom left-hand corner, is printed 'USA'. The price of the stamp, fifty cents, is printed in capital letters at the foot of the right-hand strip, the words one above the other, the letters about half the height of 'USA'.

(d) The room is square with the door in the middle of one wall. The window is opposite the door and takes up one-third of the length of the wall. Below the window and up against the wall is a square writing-table the same length as the window, with a chair at it so that I can look out of the window as I work. My single bed is against the wall to the right as you enter, i.e. it is at right angles to the wall with the door in it. The head of the bed is against the door-wall, so I can see the sky through the window when I wake up, and the bed is just over half the length of the wall. There is just enough room between the bed and the door for a small bed-side table. In the corner to the right of the window is a wash-basin. Between this and the bed is a small wardrobe. My armchair faces the centre of the room from the corner diametrically opposite the wash-basin, i.e. on the left as you enter the room. A book-case stands against the wall facing the wardrobe, and I have a hi-fi set next to it in the corner left of the window.

Write descriptions, like those above, of the following plans.

(e)

NO SMOKING

Photo

Notices

Drawing pins

Notice Board

(f)

Trees

Pond

Path

Entrance

Park

(g)

U.K. CAR BOOM   SPORT

Headlines

Columns

Photo

FLY B.A.

Advertisement

Newspaper page

(h)

Long window

Desks

Table

Chairs

Filing cabinet

Door

Office

(i)

Chair

Table

Projector

Door

Cupboard

Screen   Table   Rows of chairs
     Chair

Hall

(j)

Sales manager

Papers

Managing director

Table

Personnel manager

Papers

Carpet   Table

Candidate   Typewriter

Secretary

Interview Room

Maps

The exercises below give practice in comprehension of basic geographical expressions of position and direction. Draw and mark accurately the places and features described.

Example: The town of X is at the southernmost tip of the island, from which a road follows the coast to Y, a town halfway along the south-east coast. From Y a path rises to the peak of Mount Z in the centre of the island. Immediately to the north of Mount Z and two miles inland is an old castle. Two miles off X to the south-west is a light-house.

Answer:

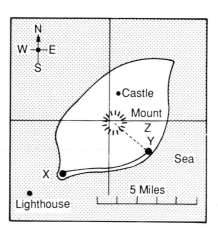

(a) In the centre of the city is the National Assembly, from where Independence Avenue goes straight to the station, at the northernmost point of the city. South of the National Assembly is People's Park, rectangular in shape and extending north to south almost to the southern limits of the city. The park is overlooked by a row of Government Ministry buildings which run alongside it on the east. Just to the west of the city is the University. Equidistant from the National Assembly, the station and the University is the Presidential Palace, just inside the city boundary. It is reached by a straight road which branches off to the left from Independence Avenue just north of the National Assembly.

(b) The capital, A, is in the centre of the broad western part of the country, and the Vaz Mountains surround it in a rough semi-circle about 20 miles away, from west to north-east. These mountains continue eastwards along the middle of the narrower part of the country for about 100 miles parallel to the coast. On the coast, south-west of A, is the port of B, which is linked to the gold mines 20 miles inland to the north by a straight road. The country's only railway goes east from A, reaches the coast after about 50 miles and follows the coast as far as the town of C, which is at the country's easternmost extremity. The town of D is half-way along the railway between A and C, and 30 miles off it is Green Island, more or less circular in shape and linked with the mainland only by air to a small airport just north-east of D.

Describe the places and features of the maps on the left below, of an
island, a city and a country, in the same way as in the exercises above,
assuming the outlines are given, as on the right.

(c)

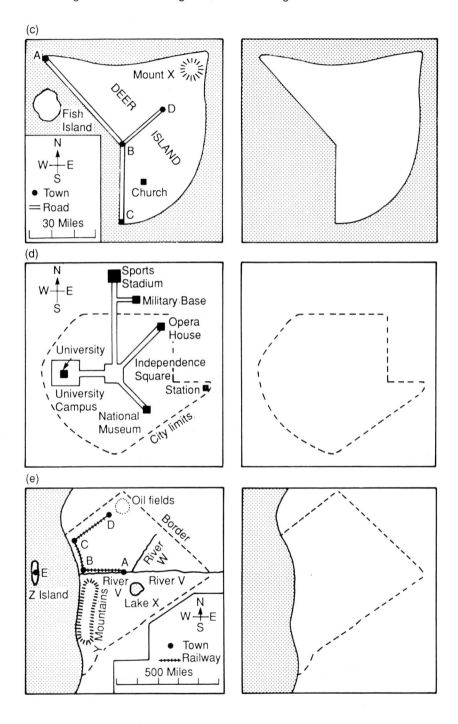

(d)

(e)

People's Appearance

Complete each passage below with the correct words from the list above it to make an accurate description of the accompanying picture.

1
cuff	formally	double-breasted
lanky	creases	button-hole
tucked	bow-tie	breast pocket
	bowler hat	

He's a tall, (a)_____ man. He's white and he's wearing a (b)_____ on his head, a dark, (c)_____ suit and a black (d)_____. An inch of (e)_____ shows from each of his sleeves. He has immaculate (f)_____ in his trousers. He has a flower in his (g)_____ and a handkerchief (h)_____ into his (i)_____. He's quite (j)_____ dressed.

2
grin	pigeon-toed	skinny
plain	bare-footed	lapels
trainers	slanting	patched
	casually	

She's a (a)_____ little kid, rather oriental-looking, with a broad (b)_____ on her face. She's wearing (c)_____ jeans and a zip-jacket with (d)_____ pockets and no (e)_____. Underneath she's wearing a (f)_____ T-shirt. From the way she's standing, she looks a bit (g)_____. She's very (h) _____ dressed. She's (i)_____ but she's carrying her shoes in her hand. They look like (j)_____.

3
hips	closely-cropped	expression
buckle	strongly-built	upright
waist	bare-headed	broad
	clean-shaven	

He's a (a)_____ black man with (b)_____ shoulders and a slim (c)_____. He has no beard or moustache; he's (d)_____. He's not wearing a hat; he's (e)_____. He has (f)_____ hair and a serious (g)_____ on his face. His trousers are held up by a belt with a large, round (h)_____. He's standing very (i)_____, with his hands on his (j)_____.

4

bow	polo-neck	slender
wavy	high-heeled	parted
teens	clasped	figure
	pleated	

She's young, still in her (a)_____. She has a (b)_____ (c)_____ and she's standing with her hands (d)_____ in front of her. Her fair, (e)_____ hair, which is (f)_____ in the middle, has a ribbon with a (g)_____ in it. She's wearing a full, knee-length (h)_____ skirt, a loose (i)_____ pullover and black, (j)_____ shoes.

5

folded	rolled up	baggy
braces	bow-legged	checked
obese	side-burns	flat cap
	thirtyish	

He's white, not very old, maybe (a)_____, and he's standing with his arms (b)_____. He's rather (c)_____, as jockeys sometimes are, and he's fat, almost (d)_____. He has a (e)_____ on, so you can't see his hair, except for his long (f)_____. He's wearing a (g)_____ shirt with the sleeves (h)_____ and a pair of (i)_____ trousers held up by (j)_____.

6 Write a brief description of each person below, referring to his or her age, character, hair, build, clothes and way of standing. Use any of the words from the exercises above and any of the following words which may be suitable.

wellingtons	beret	epaulettes	tousled
cleft chin	slim	waistcoat	lean
spectacles	single-	singlet	paunch
top hat	breasted	spotted	flared
cardigan	knock-kneed	striped	curly
stout	double-	stooped	bald
shorts	chinned	frail	

STYLE

Newspaper Headlines

Certain words are used very often in newspaper headlines because they are short or sound dramatic. Some of these words are not common in ordinary language or are used in a different sense. Headlines also omit certain words and use colloquial expressions, abbreviations and different verb tenses, e.g. STAR TO WED (A film star is going to get married).

1 For each of the following headlines find the sentence below which expresses it as it would appear in an ordinary news announcement.

'POLLS RIGGED' CHARGES
TWO SOUGHT AFTER BREAK-OUT DRAMA
CABINET RESHUFFLE URGED
SERVICE CHIEFS GAGGED: TWO QUIT
GEMS HAUL SEIZED IN SWOOP

(a) Allegations have been made that election results were falsified.
(b) Police raided a house today and took possession of jewellery stolen in a recent robbery.
(c) Police are hunting two men who made a daring escape from prison by helicopter.
(d) Senior officers of the armed forces have been instructed not to talk to the media and, as a result, two of them have resigned.
(e) Strong appeals have been made to the Prime Minister to make changes in his ministers.

2 Match each of the following words from the headlines above with its meaning below.

CHIEF   DRAMA   RESHUFFLE   GAG GEMS   SWOOP
POLL(S) QUIT   SEEK/SOUGHT   RIG   HAUL

(a) jewels
(b) goods stolen in robbery or taken by police or customs
(c) to falsify
(d) director, high-ranking officer or official
(e) raid, to raid
(f) to look for, ask for, want
(g) to silence, censor, censorship
(h) exciting, dramatic event
(i) election, voting, public opinion survey
(j) to rearrange, rearrangement (of senior jobs)
(k) to resign, leave

3 Express each of the following headlines as it would appear in an ordinary news announcement.

(a) **EDITORS URGE END TO PRESS GAG**
(b) **INDIA SEEKS US AID**
(c) **GEM SMUGGLERS CAUGHT IN PORT SWOOP**
(d) **BANK RAID CASH HAUL FOUND: 3 CHARGED**
(e) **HEAD QUITS OVER 'RIGGED' EXAM RESULTS**
(f) **RAIL CHIEFS RESHUFFLED AFTER BIG LOSSES**
(g) **GOVT DEFEATED IN POLL DRAMA**

4 For each of the following words, all frequently used in headlines, find the meaning in the list below. It will help you if you look to see how they are used in the headlines at the foot of the exercise. Then express each headline as it would appear in an ordinary news announcement.

MOVE	**CLASH**	**WOO**	**BID**	**FOIL**	**HALT**
OUST	**QUIZ**	**PLEA**	**BAN**	**BACK**	**FLEE**

(a) to prevent
(b) strong request, call for help, appeal
(c) attempt, to attempt
(d) stop, to stop
(e) to prohibit, prohibition
(f) fighting, argument, conflict, to argue, to fight

(g) support, to support
(h) to force out of office, remove from high position
(i) run away from, escape
(j) to try to attract
(k) action, step, to take action
(l) to question, interrogate

(a) **DICTATOR OUSTED: PLEA FOR CALM**
(b) **NEW MOVES TO HALT BORDER CLASHES**
(c) **GOVT BACKS ARMS BAN TO WOO LEFT**
(d) **KIDNAP BID FOILED: 3 QUIZZED, 2 FLEE**

5 Instructions as above.

SPLIT	**LEAK**	**RIDDLE**	**PROBE**	**AXE**	**LIFT**
CURB	**BAFFLED**	**STORM**	**RAP**	**CALL**	**ENVOY**

(a) mystery
(b) to escape, escape (of secret information)
(c) diplomat, ambassador
(d) close, dismiss, cancel, closure, dismissal
(e) remove (restrictions, prohibitions)
(f) criticize, reprimand

(g) at a loss to explain, mystified
(h) restrict, restriction
(i) divide, division
(j) investigate, investigation
(k) to demand, to appeal, demand, appeal
(l) angry argument

(a) **CABINET LEAK: CALL FOR PROBE**
(b) **EEC SPLIT OVER LIFTING OF TRAVEL CURBS**
(c) **DEAD ENVOY RIDDLE: YARD BAFFLED**
(d) **PM RAPS BBC IN JOBS AXE STORM**

6 Make brief headlines from the following news stories.

(a) Eighteen people were killed when the army tried to overthrow the government.
(b) A leading diplomat has been mysteriously murdered.
(c) The Prime Minister is trying to win the support of the coal miners' trade unions.
(d) The director of British Petroleum has been forced to resign.
(e) A Member of Parliament was questioned by the police in an investigation into the use of illegal drugs.

7 Express the following headlines in ordinary English.

(a) **PEER DIES IN FLATS BLAZE DRAMA**
(b) **BLAST TOLL RISING: WITNESSES SOUGHT**
(c) **COMMONS STORM OVER DEFENCE CUTS**
(d) **M-WAY DEATH CRASH: BRITON HELD**

Formal English

1 Certain established phrases are used repeatedly in the language of forms, travel conditions, regulations, advertisements and notices. Rewrite each of the following in simple English as if you were explaining the meaning to someone.

E.g. Not transferable. (rail ticket)
No one else is allowed to use this ticket.

Parental consent required if under 16. (holiday conditions)
Children under 16 must have their parents' permission.

(a) Subject to alteration. (timetable)
(b) For further information see over. (timetable)
(c) To be retained and produced on request. (rail ticket)
(d) Enter maiden name, if applicable. (official form)
(e) This portion to be given up. (theatre ticket)

(f) Complete and detach bottom section. (bank form)
(g) Affix recent photograph here. (application form)
(h) Liable to alteration without notice. (timetable)
(i) See notes overleaf. (passport application form)
(j) Insert correct amount only. (notice on automatic machine)

(k) All offers subject to availability. (chain-store gift catalogue)
(l) Services in bold type convey sleeping-cars only. (rail timetable)
(m) Delete where applicable. (official form)
(n) Enquire within. (notice in shop window)
(o) Special rates available for parties. (theatre conditions)

(p) Not valid on underground train services unless specifically stated. (travel ticket)
(q) Indicate marital status by ticking appropriate box. (official form)
(r) Non-refundable deposit payable at time of reservation. (travel agent's conditions)
(s) Expiry date. (one-week travel ticket)
(t) Insert full name of spouse. (official form)

(u) No gratuities to staff. (museum notice)
(v) Patrons are requested not to smoke. (notice in cinema)
(w) The management reserves the right of admission. (notice outside pub)
(x) All rates subject to VAT. (car hire conditions)
(y) Smokers are requested to occupy seats at the rear. (notice in bus)

2 Rewrite each of the following in simple English as if you were explaining it to someone.

E.g. You will be asked to show that adequate funds will be available to meet the cost of fees, your own maintenance and that of any dependents during your stay. (immigration regulations for students studying in Britain)

They'll ask you to show that you will have enough money to pay your college fees and to support yourself and any other members of your family you bring with you.

(a) Should there be any defect in this appliance, consult the supplier. (note with washing machine)

(b) Follow the instructions on the reverse of the form. (official form)

(c) No liability can be accepted for events beyond our control. (travel firm's rules)

(d) It should be noted that possession of the minimum entrance requirements does not guarantee admission. (university entrance regulations)

(e) Should you wish to extend your rental beyond the agreed terminating date, it is imperative that the renting station is advised immediately. (car hire conditions)

(f) The Post Office does not undertake to deliver mail to the addressee in person but to the address shown. It will be signed for by the recipient on delivery. (Post Office regulations for Registered Delivery)

(g) Normally the bank asks for seven days' notice of any withdrawals from a Deposit Account, but in emergencies you can draw immediately. (bank conditions)

(h) You will receive four tickets. Should you require more books than this at any time, extra tickets will be issued on demand. (library rules)

(i) Possession of such a letter is not obligatory but should greatly facilitate entry. (immigration regulations)

(j) A visitor can drive in Britain on a current International Driving Permit or a current domestic driving licence (which should be carried), subject to a maximum of 12 months from his last date of entry. Otherwise a British driving licence must be obtained. (driving regulations)

(k) The renter is responsible for the first £45 of each and every accident involving any damage to or loss of the vehicle during the renting period. The renter's liability may be waived by payment of a collision damage waiver fee at the rate of 95p per day. (car hire insurance rules)

(l) A caller in this country requesting a collect call will not be liable for any charges, whether or not the request for the charge to be transferred is accepted. If the request for the charge to be transferred is not accepted, the caller can elect to pay for the call himself; otherwise the call will not be established. (telephone regulations for international collect [transfer charge] calls)

3 The information below is given as if spoken informally. Rewrite each item as it would appear formally in the notice, form, printed regulations etc. indicated in brackets. Suggested beginnings are given for the first few items.

E.g. You've got to understand that we accept students only if they've got permission to study from the Home Office. (college regulations)

Students should be aware that they will be admitted to the college strictly on condition that they have obtained leave to study from the Home Office.

(a) If you want to complain, you must write a letter to the tour operator. (travel conditions)
Any complaints should be. . .

(b) If you buy anything during the sale, we won't give you your money back if you later decide you don't want it. (shop notice)
We regret that no refunds. . .

(c) Children can come in free if they're with an adult. (museum regulations)
Children will be. . .

(d) If, by chance, there's a fire, don't panic. Just leave quietly. The exits are marked on the plan at the bottom of the notice. (notice in public hall)
In the event of. . .

(e) You should go to, or phone, your embassy if you have any problems. (advice for travellers)
Travellers are advised. . .

(f) Please don't smoke. (notice in cinema)
Patrons are. . .

(g) It's important to remember that you've got to have an up-to-date visa. You can get one from the consulate. (travel regulations)
Please note that you. . .

(h) It's cheaper if you get a Certificate of Posting when you actually post your letter (the counter clerk will fill it in). You can get one later but it's more expensive. (Post Office regulations)
A Certificate of Posting may be obtained at the time of. . .

(i) There's more information on page 14. (official regulations)

(j) You can use this ticket on trains that leave after 7 in the evening. (rail ticket)

(k) These arrangements may have to be changed, particularly if the weather's bad. (travel conditions)

(l) Please keep this receipt. You may have to show it later on. (official receipt)

(m) The firm can't promise to send the goods you order until you send them the whole price. (business letter)

(n) You can do several sports here. Ask at reception if you're interested. (hotel notice)

(o) If you want a Certificate of Attendance, you'll have to show your Admission Slip. It's not absolutely necessary for you to have a teacher's note saying you come regularly, but it'll make things a lot easier. (college rules)

Colloquial English and Slang

The kind of informal English which is normal in ordinary conversation but is not considered acceptable in more formal language is called 'colloquial'. 'Slang' is even more informal language and consists mainly of particular words and phrases used principally by one group of people, eg young children, teenagers, students, professional people, working people etc. (The line between colloquial and slang words is not at all clear and many words considered colloquial by some people would be considered slang by others.) After each conversation below, first explain each colloquial or slang item listed and then rewrite the conversation in a more formal style.

E.g. Alan: Do you fancy going to the pictures tonight?
Jill: Great. Hang on, though. There's something good on telly.
(a) Do you fancy (b) Great (c) Hang on (d) telly

Answer: (a) Would you like to (b) Wonderful (c) Wait
(d) television
Alan: Would you like to go to the cinema this evening?
Jill: Wonderfui. But wait. There's a good programme on television.

1 Peter: Lend us a few quid. I'm broke.
Tony: Here's a fiver.
Peter: Smashing. Ta.

(a) us (slang)
(b) quid (slang)
(c) broke
(d) fiver
(e) smashing (slang)
(f) ta (slang)

2 George: Where's my thingumajig?
Eileen: Whatsisname's got it.

(a) thingumajig
(b) whatsisname

3 Chris: Do you like your new school?
Gus: It's OK.
Chris: And the kids in your class?
Gus: They're a decent bunch.
Chris: And the teacher?
Gus: Oh, he's a terrific bloke.

(a) OK
(b) kids
(c) decent
(d) bunch
(e) terrific
(f) bloke

4 Fred: I'm not too keen on this new guy in the office.
Alex: Yeah, he's a bit of a big-head. Throws his weight around.
Fred: Yeah, if I get any more hassle from him, I'm going to tell him what I think.
Alex: Come off it. You haven't got the guts. You'd get the sack.

(a) 'm not too keen on
(b) guy (slang)
(c) yeah (slang)
(d) big-head (slang)
(e) throws his weight around
(f) hassle
(g) come off it
(h) guts
(i) get the sack

5 Joe: Posh suit!
  Brian: My grandparents' 50th wedding anniversary. We're having a bit
       of a do.
  Joe: Come and have a drink first. On me.
  Brian: Just for a jiffy. Mustn't get there plastered.

(a) posh
(b) a do
(c) on me
(d) jiffy
(e) plastered (slang)

6 Mr Stanton: You look a bit fed up. What's up?
  Mr Moore: Someone's pinched my brolly and it's coming down in
          buckets.
  Mr Stanton: Oh, tough luck.

(a) fed up
(b) what's up?
(c) pinched
(d) brolly
(e) tough luck

7 Valerie: Saw a film the other night. Chap falls for a girl, then
         discovers she's dying. Bit of a tear-jerker. I suppose it was
         pretty corny, but I liked it. Mary Major had a part in it. She
         must be pushing 70.

(a) chap
(b) falls for
(c) tear-jerker
(d) corny
(e) pushing

8 Bob: I think my old banger's clapped out. I'll have to get a new one.
  Jim: Yes, it does look past it. What'll you get?
  Bob: I rather fancy the new Rover.
  Jim: Classy! It'll cost you a packet.

(a) banger
(b) clapped out (slang)
(c) past it
(d) fancy
(e) classy
(f) packet (slang)

9 Donald: Someone's walked off with my specs!
  Sheila: Don't be daft. You've got them in your hand.
  Donald: Oh, yes. I'm going bonkers.

(a) walked off with
(b) specs
(c) daft
(d) bonkers (slang)

10 Philip: I'm afraid the new secretary's a dead loss, John. The red-
         head with the trendy clothes.
  John: You're right. She thinks she's the cat's whiskers, but in actual
       fact she's a bit dim.
  Philip: Yes, her work's poor and, as you say, she fancies herself. She's
        very snooty with the other girls.
  John: Do you think we ought to give her the push?
  Philip: I'm afraid so, but she'll be shattered.

(a) dead loss (slang)
(b) trendy (slang)
(c) cat's whiskers (slang)
(d) dim
(e) fancies herself
(f) snooty
(g) give her the push (slang)
(h) shattered

English in Advertising

Trade Names

1 Many British firms and shops choose a short name which attracts attention, is easy to remember and immediately identifies the service being offered. This name is often spelt in a kind of simple phonetic spelling to make it even more unique and memorable, e.g. EAZIWASH (easy wash) is a launderette and FIZZEEK (physique) is a gymnasium and health club.

On the left below are the real names of fourteen British firms or shops. Give the normal spelling of each and find on the right the kind of business it is.

(a)	LITE BITE	photo-processing shop
(b)	SHUSELLA	photo-copying firm
(c)	KEEP-A-KREASE	children's clothes shop
(d)	SUPASNAPS	snack bar
(e)	KWICK KOPY	shoe-shop
(f)	KWALITY FASHIONS	dry cleaners
(g)	KUMFY KIDDY WEAR	taxi firm
(h)	HANDICARS	garage and repair shop
(i)	MR KLEEN	women's clothes shop
(j)	SNAX	dry cleaners
(k)	MOTOR KARE	hairdressers
(l)	LOOKRITE	snack bar
(m)	FLITE CENTRE	car-hire firm
(n)	U-DRIVE	travel agency

2 Products are often named in the same way as the businesses above. Give the normal spelling of each real product on the left below and find on the right what kind of product it is.

(a)	KLEENOFF	beds
(b)	KATTOMEAT	video and audio home entry system
(c)	ANSAFONE	cleaning fluids
(d)	SUPALOK	bathroom equipment
(e)	RESTRITE	rucksacks
(f)	KARRIMOR	strong glue
(g)	INSTAFLOW	telephone answering machines
(h)	ANSADOR	pet food

3 Some British firms use normal spelling in their names but form them by combining two words into one. What kind of business do the following real firms do?

(a)	TRANSLAGENCY	(e)	QUICK-LETS
(b)	AUTOCHECK	(f)	FIGURETRIM
(c)	AUTOPASS	(g)	SUNTOURS
(d)	SECURICOR	(h)	DATAFLOW

Puns

A pun is a humorous use of a word or phrase which has two meanings or of two words or phrases which look or sound similar. Puns are used not only in jokes but in many forms of publicity because they catch the eye and amuse. Explain the following puns by giving the two possible meanings (often one meaning is literal and the other figurative).

E.g.: WHEN YOU DECIDE TO GIVE HER A RING, GIVE US A RING (Advertisement for a jeweller's shop)

Explanation: 'To give someone a ring' means, literally, 'to give a wedding or engagement ring' or, figuratively, 'to telephone'.

E.g.: WHAT TO GIVE YOUR FAMILY FOR LUNCH? SAY 'CHEESE'! (Advertisement for cheese)

Explanation: In addition to its literal meaning of asking for cheese when buying food, the last phrase is often used by someone taking a photograph to make the subject smile.

(a) FOR A FEW POUNDS YOU CAN LOSE A FEW (Advertisement for a slimming course)
(b) GO UP IN THE WORLD (Advertisement to recruit air stewards and stewardesses)
(c) WE'LL GIVE YOU SOUND ADVICE (Hi-fi shop advertisement)
(d) WE OFFER YOU A GOOD DEAL (Bank advertisement to attract new customers)
(e) HAVE YOU THOUGHT ABOUT BUYING OUR NEW BED? SLEEP ON IT (Advertisement for a new bed)
(f) IT'S NOT WORTH DYING FOR A DRINK (Advertisement warning of the dangers of alcoholism)
(g) YOUR VIEWS ARE REFLECTED IN THE MIRROR (Advertisement for The *Mirror* newspaper)
(h) MAKE A SNAP DECISION (Advertisement for a new camera)
(i) MONEY MATTERS (Title of the financial section of a newspaper)
(j) IT'S GOOD FOR YOU, NATURALLY (Advertisement for fruit juice)
(k) GO BY AIR. IT'S PLANE COMMON SENSE (Advertisement for air travel)
(l) WE'LL GIVE YOU RED-CARPET TREATMENT (OR BLUE, OR GREEN, OR BROWN, OR YELLOW. . .) (Carpet shop advertisement)
(m) SEA FOR YOURSELF (Advertisement to attract recruits to the Royal Navy)
(n) TRY OUR GLUE ONCE AND YOU'LL ALWAYS STICK WITH US (Advertisement for a brand of glue)
(o) CHRISTMAS IS A TIME TO THINK OF FAMILY TIES. BUY OURS. (Advertisement for men's ties)
(p) NEXT TIME YOU WANT TO BE AT YOUR BEST FOR A SPECIAL OCCASION, CONSIDER BUYING A PRODUCT OF THE AROMATA COMPANY (IT MAKES SCENTS) (Perfume advertisement)
(q) THE WEATHER-MEN CAN'T GUARANTEE YOU AN INDIAN SUMMER, BUT WE CAN (Travel agency advertisement)
(r) WE'LL GIVE YOU FOOD FOR THOUGHT (Restaurant advertisement)

SPOKEN ENGLISH

Forms of Spoken Address

How do British people address each other? What do they call each other? Complete the spoken phrases at the end of each sentence below with a word or phrase from the following list. In some cases two or even three items could be used. If no particular form of address is normally used, write nothing. Some of the words in the list are used more than once, and some are not used in any of the phrases.

E.g. Department store assistant to woman customer: Can I help you, _____?
  Answer: madam
  Parents to their child: What are you doing, _____?
  Answer: dear, love or darling
  Rail traveller to ticket-clerk: Return to Lancaster, please, _____.
  Answer: nothing

grandma	officer	viewers	ladies and gentlemen
sir	caller	gentleman	Your Majesty
mum	men	listeners	men and women
mister	my friend	grannie	daddy
grandad	madam	dear	
darling	love	dad	
mate	grandpa	mummy	

(a) Child to his or her mother: Can I go out, _____?
(b) Telephone operator: Please hold the line, _____.
(c) Television presenter to people watching at home: Welcome to the Saturday Night Show, _____.
(d) Child to his or her grandfather: Thank you for the present, _____.
(e) Someone to a bank-clerk or librarian: Can you help me, _____?
(f) Someone making a formal speech to his audience: I'll try to be brief, _____.
(g) Polite shop-assistant to male customer: Can I help you, _____?
(h) Someone to the Queen: Good evening, _____.
(i) Customer to a shop-assistant: Can I try on this coat, _____?
(j) Wife to her husband: You look tired, _____.
(k) Radio presenter to people at home: Now we have a surprise for you, _____.
(l) Workman to a man passing by: What's the time, _____?
(m) Policeman to a man who asks for help: Yes, _____.
(n) Policeman to a woman who asks for help: Yes, _____.
(o) Someone to a policeman: Excuse me, _____.
(p) Child to his or her grandmother: Here are your glasses, _____.
(q) Woman shopkeeper in a small, friendly shop to a customer: What would you like, _____?
(r) Soldier to his commanding officer: Can I go, _____?
(s) Commanding officer to his soldiers: I want more effort, _____.
(t) Child to his or her father: Goodnight, _____.
(u) Someone to a stranger in the street: Excuse me, _____.

Colloquial Responses

On the right in the exercises below are some common colloquial responses, i.e. phrases often used in particular, informal situations. Of course, different people respond in different ways, but the phrases below are very common.

1 For each spoken item on the left below find the most natural response on the right.

(a) You mustn't tell a soul.	Dump it anywhere.
(b) Where shall I put your case?	Care for a spin?
(c) Can I bring a friend to your party?	My lips are sealed.
(d) People say you're very generous.	Flattery will get you nowhere.
(e) I like your new car.	The more the merrier.

2 Instructions as above.

(a) How did you know I was going out with Jenny?	Well, boys will be boys.
(b) I thought you were going to accept the offer.	Beggars can't be choosers.
(c) Bobby's in trouble at school.	I'm having second thoughts.
(d) I'm afraid this is the only job I can offer you.	Well, you can't win them all.
(e) I didn't get the job.	A little bird told me.

3 Instructions as above.

(a) How shall we decide?	I'm afraid I haven't a clue.
(b) I've got a coin.	Let's toss for it.
(c) Do you know where the cinema is?	Let me sleep on it.
(d) We need a decision soon.	Oh, it's on the tip of my tongue.
(e) Do you know what it's called?	OK. You toss, I'll call. Tails!

4 Instructions as above.

(a) Cheers!	I could do with one.
(b) Can I have some more meat?	Oh, this is on me.
(c) I'll buy the drinks.	Help yourself.
(d) Cup of tea?	Cheers!
(e) I don't think I can afford this restaurant. It looks a bit expensive.	No, it's my round.

5 Instructions as above.

(a) Can I use your phone?	Yes, by the skin of my teeth.
(b) Our plan's a failure. It won't work.	If you don't mind taking pot luck.
(c) Did you catch the train?	Every little helps.
(d) Can I come to lunch?	Back to square one.
(e) Sorry I can't make a bigger donation.	Be my guest.

6 Instructions as above.

(a) I've got some news.   OK. Thanks all the same.
(b) I hope the weather's good for   Well, it can't be helped.
      our trip tomorrow.
(c) He's a very odd chap.   I'm all ears.
(d) I've left our tickets at home!   It takes all sorts.
(e) Sorry I can't help you.   I'm keeping my fingers crossed.

In the following exercises, the situations are very informal, e.g. between very close friends, when we sometimes use very casual, ironic or even rude responses.

7 Instructions as above.

(a) Can you lend me £100?   Serves you right.
(b) I've eaten too much. I feel ill.   OK. Suit yourself.
(c) Where were you last night?   That'll be the day.
(d) I think I'd rather go to a pub.   You must be joking.
(e) I'll pay you back soon.   Mind your own business.

8 Instructions as above.

(a) Why don't you do some work?   Have it your own way.
(b) I insist on doing it like this.   How should I know?
(c) Where's Ann tonight?   I like that!
(d) I've borrowed your coat.   Rather you than me.
(e) It's very cold, but I'm going for   I can't be bothered.
      a walk.

9 Instructions as above.

(a) You won't succeed without   I couldn't care less.
      hard work, you know.
(b) You don't seem worried about   I don't get it.
      smoking so much.
(c) Well, OK. Maybe you're right.   Stop preaching.
      We'll go to the party. And I'll
      lend you the money you
      asked me for.
(d) Sorry I was so long on the   Now you're talking.
      phone. Now we'll be late for
      the film.
(e) That's the joke. Don't you   Yes, thanks to you.
      think it's funny?

Exclamations

1 People often react to certain situations by using sounds rather than real words, and people from different countries often use different sounds, e.g. British people often say 'ouch!' when they feel a sudden pain, whereas other nationalities sometimes say 'aie!' Of course different British people will have different responses, but the following are common.

Answer the questions below with sounds from the following list.

giddyup!	**eh? (rhymes with 'say')**	**mm!**
whoah!	**wow! (rhymes with 'how')**	**sh!**
whoops!	**boo! (rhymes with 'too')**	**well?**
there, there		

What do you say if you. . .

(a) . . . want someone to be quiet?
(b) . . . don't catch what a friend says?
(c) . . . want a horse to start or go faster?
(d) . . . comfort a child in pain and crying?
(e) . . . jump out from behind a tree to surprise someone?
(f) . . . suddenly lose your balance, or drop something?
(g) . . . are waiting for someone to answer your question?
(h) . . . are suddenly impressed by something?
(i) . . . want a horse to slow down or stop?
(j) . . . express spontaneous delight!

2 Instructions as above.

hear, hear	**er (rhymes with 'sir')**	**gosh!**
now, now	**hi! (rhymes with 'lie')**	**ta-ta**
tut-tut	**oi! (rhymes with 'boy')**	**ta**
cheers		

What do you say if you. . .

(a) . . . thank a friend casually?
(b) . . . hesitate or forget something?
(c) . . . calm an over-excited, angry friend?
(d) . . . and a friend raise your glasses to drink together?
(e) . . . say goodbye casually to a friend?
(f) . . . express your agreement with something said in a speech?
(g) . . . greet a friend casually?
(h) . . . see someone trying to steal your bag?
(i) . . . express disapproval about something you see or hear?
(j) . . . express surprise?

Spoken Numbers and Measurements

1   The sentences below are written as they would be spoken. Rewrite them as they would normally be written, using numbers and abbreviated forms.

E.g.   I take a size fourteen and a half shirt.
I take a size 14½ shirt.

Ten per cent of the working population earn less than six thousand, five hundreds pounds a year.
10% of the working population earn less than £6,500 a year.

(a) Forty minus fifteen plus six is thirty-one.
(b) Eighty-one divided by three is twenty-seven.
(c) Three times six is eighteen.
(d) Queen Elizabeth the First reigned from fifteen fifty-eight to sixteen oh three.
(e) The show is due to commence at seven thirty p.m. on the second of August.
(f) It cost me six pounds seventy-five pence.
(g) Phone me any time on four double-one four eight five oh.
(h) Please note that our reference number is double-four dash seven stroke five oh nine.
(i) The total cost is estimated at two million, four hundred and seventy-one thousand, eight hundred and fifty pounds.
(j) The mixture is two thirds water.
(k) A litre is one point seven six pints.
(l) Twenty-two per cent of the candidates passed with distinction.
(m) The temperature was thirty degrees centigrade, that is eighty-six degrees fahrenheit.
(n) It measures four feet two and three quarter inches by two feet eight and a half inches.
(o) France beat England three nil. (football)
(p) Brazil and Italy drew three all. (football)
(q) The score stands at thirty love to Becker. (tennis)

2   Write out the following sentences exactly as they would be spoken, i.e. as in the exercise above.

(a) $73 + 20 - 43 = 50$
(b) $129 \div 3 = 43$
(c) $4 \times 21 = 84$
(d) Edward VII died in 1910.
(e) It was exactly 11.35 a.m. on 21st May.
(f) They cost £3.25 each.
(g) Our new phone number is 307 2201.
(h) Please quote reference no. 8/2-771.
(i) The population is 3,255,840.
(j) I am ⅛ French.
(k) 1 mile = 1.609 kilometres.
(l) It is 17.38% gold.
(m) Water freezes at 32 °F, ie 0 °C.
(n) The picture measured 2′6½″ × 5′8¼″.
(o) We won 3:0. (football)
(p) The final score was 2:2. (football)
(q) The score's 15:0 to me at the moment. (tennis)

Well-Known Spoken Phrases

The following common phrases are associated with particular situations. Identify each phrase by describing briefly who would say it and in what circumstances.

E.g. 'Please fasten your safety-belts.'
Air-stewardess to passengers before take-off or landing.

(a) 'Mind the doors!'
(b) 'To eat here or take away?'
(c) 'Many happy returns.'
(d) 'How do you plead?'
(e) 'Just a trim, please.'
(f) 'Have you anything to declare?'
(g) 'Heel!'
(h) 'Take this prescription and come back and see me in a week.'
(i) 'I'm putting you through.'
(j) 'A pint of bitter, please.'
(k) 'Going. . . going. . . gone!'
(l) 'Here's to the bride and groom.'
(m) 'I now pronounce you man and wife.'
(n) 'I swear to tell the truth, the whole truth and nothing but the truth.'
(o) 'This won't hurt.'
(p) 'God bless her and all who sail in her.'
(q) 'Amen.'
(r) 'Once upon a time. . . '
(s) 'Say "Cheese".'
(t) 'All aboard!.'
(u) 'Man overboard!'

MISCELLANEOUS

Geo-political Names

1 Explain the difference between the two names in each of the following pairs.

(a) England and (Great) Britain
(b) (Great) Britain and the United Kingdom
(c) (Great) Britain and the British Isles
(d) Europe and Continental Europe
(e) The Middle East and the Far East
(f) India and the Indian Subcontinent
(g) America and North America
(h) South America and Latin America
(i) The Arctic and the Antarctic
(j) Australia and Australasia
(k) South Africa and Southern Africa

2 Explain the difference between the two adjectives in each of the following pairs.

(a) Arab and Arabic
(b) Scottish and Scotch
(c) Oriental and Occidental

3 Match each country on the left below with the name on the right by which it is also known.

(a) Holland	Eire
(b) Iran	The Federal Republic of Germany
(c) West Germany	The Netherlands
(d) East Germany	Ulster
(e) Sri Lanka	Persia
(f) The Republic of Ireland	Ceylon
(g) Northern Ireland	The German Democratic Republic

4 Which countries are referred to by the following expressions?

(a) The Common Market countries
(b) The (British) Commonwealth
(c) The NATO countries
(d) The Warsaw Pact countries
(e) The West Indies
(f) The Gulf States
(g) The Superpowers
(h) The Third World

5 Which countries are sometimes referred to by the following colloquial expressions?

(a) The States
(b) Down Under
(c) The Land of the Rising Sun
(d) The Emerald Isle

6 For each country below give i) the adjective and ii) the word describing the person who comes from that country.

Eg	China	i) Chinese	ii) a Chinese
	Poland	i) Polish	ii) a Pole
	Wales	i) Welsh	ii) a Welshman/Welshwoman

(a) Pakistan	(h) New Zealand	(o) Finland
(b) Peru	(i) Lebanon	(p) Belgium
(c) Thailand	(j) Denmark	(q) Ireland
(d) Scotland	(k) Holland	(r) Bangladesh
(e) Turkey	(l) England	(s) Portugal
(f) Philippines	(m) Iraq	(t) France
(g) Sweden	(n) Spain	(u) Greece

7 Inhabitants of London, Cairo and Washington are called Londoners, Cairenes and Washingtonians. Of which cities are the following people inhabitants?

(a) Parisians	(e) Neapolitans	(i) Liverpudlians
(b) Chicagoans	(f) Aberdonians	(j) Viennese
(c) Venetians	(g) Milanese	(k) Muscovites
(d) Mancunians	(h) Glaswegians	(l) Romans

Names and Titles

1 Put each of the following words and phrases in its correct place in the sentences below.

surname   pen-name hyphenated name (or 'double-barrelled name')
stage name pet name Christian name
nickname   alias   maiden name

(a) My name is Bob Jones. Of course 'Jones' is my _____.
(b) Bob, short for 'Robert', is my _____.
(c) At school the other boys called me 'Brains'. It was my _____.
(d) As a criminal I used the false name 'Fred Yates'. That was my

_____.

(e) When I write novels I call myself Simon Sims. That's my _____.
(f) Some people have two parts to their family name, e.g. Mr Smith-Stewart. This is called a _____.
(g) I was Miss North before I married, so 'North' is my _____.
(h) My wife affectionately calls me 'Dimple'. It's a kind of _____.
(i) As an actress in the theatre I was known as Gloria Gold. That was my _____.

2

Ms Louise Manners	**W.G. Smithson Esq.**
Mrs P. Tucker M.P.	**Sir Robin Sawyer**
Jones Bros.	**Rev. Graham Lee**
G.L. Cousins M.A.	**John Fox O.B.E.**
Adm.V.E.Nott R.N. (ret)	**W.P.C. Lockwood**
Z. Wilkins R.A.	**H.R.H. The Prince of Wales**

Answer the following questions from the list of people above.

(a) Who used to be a high-ranking naval officer?
(b) Who is in the police force?
(c) Who has a university degree?
(d) Who prefers not to state whether she is married?
(e) Who is a priest?
(f) Who has received a knighthood?
(g) Who sits in the House of Commons?
(h) Who is formally addressed on an envelope?

(i)   Who has a royal title?
(j)   Which members of a family run a business together?
(k)   Who is a recognized artist?
(l)   Who has received an honour from the King or Queen?

3   Give the full names for which the following are the common short forms.

(a) Dick   (d) Bert   (g) Tom   (j) Tricia
(b) Ted   (e) Andy   (h) Bob   (k) Jenny
(c) Bill   (f) Tony   (i) Liz   (l) Maggie

Give the common short forms of the following names.

(m) James   (p) Christopher   (s) Leslie   (v) Catherine
(n) Gerald   (q) Joseph   (t) Frederick   (w) Susan
(o) Michael   (r) Harold   (u) Pamela   (x) Diana

Foreign Words and Phrases

A great many expressions used in English come originally from other languages but most of them are now so absorbed into English that they are no longer thought of as foreign. However, some words and phrases, like those in the following exercises, have retained their original spelling, pronunciation and foreign identity.

1   FRENCH Put each of the following expressions into its correct place in the sentences below.

tête-à-tête	**hors d'oeuvre**	**cul-de-sac**	**bon voyage**
rendezvous	**blasé**	**carte blanche**	**grand prix**
nouveaux riches	**chic**		

(a) The advantage of living in a _____ is that there is no through traffic, so it's very quiet.
(b) Let's order. I'm hungry. I'm going to start with a nice _____.
(c) The boss didn't tell me how he wanted the project carried out. He gave me _____ to do it as I thought best.
(d) The French _____ was won by a Brazilian driver in an Italian car.
(e) _____, and send us a post-card when you arrive!
(f) She chooses her clothes, hair-style and make-up so that she is in the latest fashion. She always looks very _____.
(g) I have one or two ideas I'd like to discuss with you. Could we have a little _____ one day soon?
(h) He was very excited when his first book was published, but now, having written over 30, he's fairly _____ about it.
(i) That restaurant is a favourite _____ for writers and artists.
(j) A snob tends to look down on _____ as people who have money but no class or taste.

2   FRENCH Instructions as above.

encore	**bloc**	**début**	**c'est la vie**
gourmet	**façade**	**détente**	**avant garde**
coup	**entourage**		

(a) If we take Charles out to dinner, we must choose a good restaurant. He's a _____.

(b) There was a successful _____ last night. The president has been arrested and the main government buildings are in the hands of the army.

(c) Film stars don't usually travel alone. They're normally surrounded by a large _____ of agents, secretaries and other helpers.

(d) The audience liked her songs so much that at the end they shouted, '_____', and she obliged by singing one more.

(e) Yes, I've had some bad luck recently, but it's no use worrying about it. _____.

(f) The term 'Eastern _____ countries' refers to the Soviet Union and the other socialist states of Eastern Europe.

(g) He's a very _____ artist. I have no idea what he's trying to express. Very few people understand his paintings.

(h) She made her _____ as an actress in a film at the age of 14.

(i) That building still has its old _____ as you can see, but the rest of the building behind it has been rebuilt and modernized.

(j) At the moment there is a _____ between the two countries. Relations are much easier.

3 LATIN Instructions as above.

status quo	**ad nauseam**	**ego**	**persona non**
per capita	**post mortem**	**curriculum**	**grata**
vice versa	**pro rata**	**vitae**	
bona fide			

(a) Duty-free goods may be purchased only by _____ travellers. Please show your flight-ticket when buying.

(b) Applicants for this post should write enclosing a detailed _____.

(c) Rental rates for our cars are £50 a day. Longer periods will be charged _____ with no reductions, so a one-week rental will be £350.

(d) He was barred from this country in 1985 and has been _____ ever since.

(e) Everyone must do what *she* wants, listen to what *she* says, go where *she* decides to go. No one else is important. She really has got a big _____.

(f) Some people just want to preserve the _____ in this country, but others want change, reform, development.

(g) A great many British people spend their holidays in America, and _____.

(h) The _____ examination showed that she died of cancer.

(i) Canada has a _____ income of about $17,000.

(j) I'm afraid he's rather a boring person. He goes on and on _____ about his political views.

4 MIXED Instructions as above.

siesta	(Spanish)	kindergarten	(German)
macho	(Spanish)	incognito	(Italian)
patio	(Spanish)	bravo	(Italian)
blitz	(German)	graffiti	(Italian)
kaput	(German)	kowtow	(Chinese)

(a) A man who is very hard, tough and masculine is sometimes described as '_____'.

(b) At the age of three she went to a _____ just to learn to play with other children.

(c) After lunch I like to have a _____ for an hour or so.

(d) A week after the wall was repainted, it was covered with _____ again.

(e) My television's _____. I'll have to buy a new one.

(f) You performed very well. _____!

(g) He didn't want to be recognized so he changed his appearance and travelled _____.

(h) My garden was looking very overgrown and neglected so I did a real _____ on it last Saturday. I worked all day.

(i) When the Prime Minister comes, just be polite and normal. There's no need to _____ to him.

(j) No, our house hasn't got a proper garden, just a paved _____.

Homophones

A homophone is a word which has exactly the same pronunciation as another word although the spelling and meaning are different.

E.g. One – won   nose – knows
write – right   piece – peace

1 Write a homophone for each of the following words.

(a)	two	(g)	wear	(m)	bored	(s)	meet
(b)	eye	(h)	war	(n)	seize	(t)	past
(c)	guest	(i)	here	(o)	principal	(u)	blue
(d)	waste	(j)	pair	(p)	caught	(v)	red
(e)	male	(k)	wait	(q)	hole	(w)	stairs
(f)	way	(l)	steel	(r)	sale	(x)	born

2 Instructions as above.

(a)	road	(g)	miner	(m)	berry	(s)	heard
(b)	so	(h)	died	(n)	higher	(t)	sent
(c)	rain	(i)	sort	(o)	through	(u)	sell
(d)	sweet	(j)	pause	(p)	morning	(v)	course
(e)	fair	(k)	main	(q)	praise	(w)	tire
(f)	bold	(l)	pale	(r)	ceiling	(x)	idle

Abbreviations

1 For each abbreviation on the left below find another on the right which has something in common with it.

(a) a.m.	Cantab.
(b) PC	BA
(c) Oxon.	PM
(d) MP	p.m.
(e) BR	CID
(f) RN	BST
(g) GMT	RAF
(h) BBC	BC
(i) AD	IBA

2 For each abbreviation on the left below there is another in the centre and another on the right which together make a group of three abbreviations which have something in common. Make as many groups of three as you can.

(a) NHS	ft	WHO
(b) oz	Rd	Ave
(c) in	GP	PhD
(d) Con.	MA	yd
(e) St	lb	st
(f) BA	mph	SLD
(g) mpg	Lab.	cc

3 Put each of the following abbreviations in its correct place in the sentences below.

SOS	**TUC**	**QC**	**VIP**
UFO	**IQ**	**VC**	**PLO**
CND	**HQ**	**MBE**	**DIY**

(a) The United Nations _____ is in New York.

(b) Now then all you _____ fans. Here's an all-purpose tool to help you in a hundred ways to do those home repairs.

(c) Although he was defended by an eminent _____, he was found guilty and sent to prison for eight years.

(d) He's extremely bright. They say he has an _____ of 160.

(e) He was the only soldier in the regiment to win the _____ in the Second World War.

(f) The _____ represents the great majority of working men and women in Britain.

(g) The aim of the _____ is to establish a permanent home for the Palestinian people.

(h) Film-stars, prime ministers and other celebrities are entertained in the special _____ lounge at the airport.

(i) The Beatles each received an honour from the Queen. It was the _____.

(j) Their _____ was picked up on the radio by two other ships and a plane. They were rescued within hours.

(k) Some people thought the object in the sky was a _____ bringing visitors from another planet but it turned out to be a small plane.

(l) _____ will support any moves to abolish or reduce nuclear weapons.

4 Some abbreviations, like the following, are pronounced as one word. Put each one in its correct place in the sentences below.

UNESCO	**VAT**	**NASA**
AIDS	**NATO**	**OPEC**

(a) The price is £87 but it's subject to _____ so that will be £95.70.
(b) _____ has been described as possibly the most deadly epidemic in the history of the world.
(c) _____ has announced that the next space shuttle launch will take place in August.
(d) The _____ nations are to meet in Geneva to decide whether to increase the price of oil.
(e) _____ military exercises involving American forces will be held in Britain and West Germany this winter.
(f) An expert from _____ produced a report on primary education in underdeveloped countries.

Similes

1 Put the following words into the correct spaces in the sentences below.

sandboy	**hills**	**sheet**	**new pin**
feather	**knife**	**dust**	**flash**

(a) I've heard that story a hundred times before. It's as old as the _____.
(b) Her children are always beautifully dressed and as clean as a _____.
(c) I'm afraid I find ancient history as dry as _____.
(d) What's wrong? Are you ill? You're as white as a _____.
(e) She went on a diet, lost several kilos and now she's as light as a _____.
(f) The schoolchildren were very bright. They answered my questions as quick as a _____.
(g) He loves cars. When he's repairing his car, he's as happy as a _____.
(h) He's very intelligent and quick-thinking. He's as sharp as a _____.

2 Put the correct adjectives from the following list into the sentences below.

cool	**sober**	**good**	**poor**
thin	**deaf**	**drunk**	**fit**

(a) He was as _____ as a lord.
(b) I was as _____ as a judge.
(c) He's as _____ as a church mouse.
(d) She remained as _____ as a cucumber.
(e) The children were as _____ as gold.
(f) He's as _____ as a rake.
(g) I'm as _____ as a fiddle.
(h) He's as _____ as a post.

Proverbs

1 Match each of the following common proverbs with the most appropriate situation from the list below.

(a) Actions speak louder than words.
(b) Don't look a gift horse in the mouth.
(c) When in Rome, do as the Romans.
(d) Don't count your chickens before they're hatched.
(e) Blood is thicker than water.
(f) Prevention is better than cure.
(g) One good turn deserves another.
(h) Make hay while the sun shines.

1) Yes, you'll probably pass the exam, but don't depend on it till you hear the result.
2) Make the most out of life while you can, while you're young and without any big responsibilities.
3) Well, the cassette recorder he gave you may have a few defects, but you shouldn't complain. It cost you nothing.
4) I'm not impressed by fine speeches. Why doesn't the government *do* something?
5) Don't wait till you've got flu. Try not to catch it.
6) If you're in a foreign country, you should get used to the customs there.
7) I'll probably lose my job by going there to help him, but he's in trouble and he *is* my brother.
8) Yes, of course I'll help you. *You* lent *me* a hand last week.

2 Instructions as above.

(a) Nothing venture, nothing gain.
(b) It never rains but it pours.
(c) Once bitten, twice shy.
(d) A bad workman blames his tools.
(e) Too many cooks spoil the broth.
(f) It's no use crying over spilt milk.
(g) Pride comes before a fall.
(h) Absence makes the heart grow fonder.

1) Well, it's a pity but it's in the past now and there's nothing we can do about it.
2) Oh, my God, I've got tickets for the wrong day *and* they ruined my suit at the cleaners *and* my wallet was stolen *and* I forgot my wife's birthday!
3) My wife's spending a week with her parents. I do miss her.
4) I'm not investing my money in that company again. I lost everything last time I did.
5) Ask her out to dinner. If you don't, you'll never know if she likes you.
6) He was over-confident. He thought he couldn't go wrong, but then he got complacent and failed the all-important exam.
7) Do we really need so many of us to do this job? Won't we get in each other's way?
8) It's not my fault I haven't finished this typing yet. It's not a very good machine and the stuff I have to copy is very difficult to read.

Euphemisms

To avoid referring too directly to unpleasant, embarrassing or personal matters we often prefer to use more indirect words or phrases, which are called euphemisms.

1 Rewrite the following sentences, replacing the euphemisms, in italics, with more simple, direct words or phrases.

(a) I'm afraid Mrs Wild *passed away* last night.
(b) Excuse me, where's the nearest *public convenience*?
(c) *Senior citizens* are entitled to free bus travel.
(d) Sadly, my grandmother is *no longer with us*.
(e) In the middle of the exam I had to *answer a call of nature*.
(f) His hat *had seen better days*.
(g) We had to have our dog *put to sleep*.

The following sentences are very direct. Rewrite them, replacing the parts in italics with euphemisms.

E.g. She's *very old*.
      She's not as young as she was/getting on/advanced in years.

(a) He's *fat and ugly*.
(b) I'm going to *vomit*.
(c) She's *a terrible cook*.
(d) You were *drunk* last night.
(e) This work *is very careless*.
(f) Grandpa *can hardly walk*.

2 Instructions as in the first exercise above.

(a) We were obliged to *dispense with Miss Farr's services* last month.
(b) He has been asked to leave the country due to his involvement with *activities incompatible with his diplomatic duties here*.
(c) The state has an obligation to assist *the less privileged members of the community*.
(d) The estate agent says the house *needs some attention*.
(e) The ambassador said the talks were likely to *have a negative outcome*.
(f) Tourists are advised to avoid the *less salubrious* parts of the city.
(g) Mr West *has shown insufficient effort* in the execution of his duties.

Instructions as in the second exercise above.

(a) Your representative *lied* to us.
(b) The talks were *a waste of time*.
(c) He's *always late for work*.
(d) Your product is *very badly-made*.
(e) Our relations with your country *are awful*.
(f) It would be *stupid* to *go on strike* now.
(g) *You owe us money*.
(h) We were *very angry* with your letter.

Britain

The election system

Put each of the following words or phrases in its correct place in the passage below.

proportional representation	**polling day**	**by-election**
Member of Parliament	**canvassing**	**eligible**
call an election	**secret ballot**	**deposit**
House of Commons	**constituents**	**campaigns**
stand for election	**constituencies**	**turn-out**
General Election	**polling stations**	

Middleford. Election Result. No. of registered voters: 100,000

Mr G. Smith (Labour)	30,000 votes
Mrs R. Green (Conservative)	25,000 votes
Miss L. Jones (Independent)	10,000 votes
Mr W. Woods (Communist)	5,000 votes

A (a)_____ has just taken place all over the United Kingdom. These must take place every five years unless the Prime Minister decides to (b)_____ earlier. Above is the result in Middleford, one of the approximately 635 (c)_____ into which the country is divided for this purpose. (d)_____ was last Thursday, when the election (e)_____ and door-to-door (f)_____ stopped and the people of Middleford went to the (g)_____ to make their choice, in a (h)_____, from the four candidates (anyone over the age of 21 can (i)_____, on payment of a (j)_____ of £500, which is returned if he or she receives at least 5% of the votes cast). Voting is not compulsory and the number of people (k)_____ to vote in Middleford (everyone over 18) was 100,000, so the (l)_____ was 70%. Now Mr Smith will become the (m)_____ for Middleford, which means he will represent the people of Middleford in the (n)_____ in London. If he should die or be forced to give up his seat, the people of Middleford will have to vote again, in a (o)_____ to replace him. It is a very simple system and Mr Smith will try to represent all his (p)_____ fairly, whether they voted for him or not. However, the fact remains that most voters in Middleford voted for candidates (and parties) other than Mr Smith, and their votes are now lost. It is seats which are important in Parliament, not votes, and it is easy to see why the smaller parties would like a system of (q)_____, in which the number of votes they won was reflected in the number of seats they received in Parliament.

The House of Commons

1 Put each of the following words or phrases in its correct place in the passage below.

Cabinet	**benches**	**Foreign Secretary**
backbenchers	**Budget**	**Shadow Cabinet**
Prime Minister	**Speaker**	**Home Secretary**
ministers	**front bench**	**Leader of the Opposition**
debates	**Opposition**	**Chancellor of the Exchequer**

This is the House of Commons, where Members of Parliament take their seats on the green leather (a)_____ according to their party and position. One of them is chosen to be the (b)_____, who acts as a kind of chairman of the (c)_____ which take place in the House. In front of him on his right sit the MPs of the biggest party, which forms the government, and facing them sit the MPs of the parties who oppose them, the (d)_____. The leaders of these two groups sit at the front on each side. MPs without special positions in their parties sit behind their leaders at the back. They are called (e)_____. The leader of the government, the (f)_____, sits on the government (g)_____, of course, next to his or her (h)_____. The most important of these form the (i)_____. The minister responsible for relations with other countries is called the (j)_____. The one responsible for law and security is called the (k)_____. The one who deals with financial matters and prepares the annual (l)_____ speech on the economic state of the country is called the (m)_____. Opposite this group sits the (n)_____ (the main person in the largest party opposing the government) and the (o)_____, each member of which specializes in a particular area of government.

2 The picture below shows a view of the House of Commons from the Public Gallery. After completing the exercise above, match each of the following people or groups of people with a letter on the picture.

backbenchers   **Government**   **Leader of the Opposition**
Cabinet   **Prime Minister** **Shadow Cabinet**
Opposition   **Speaker**

Famous places
The following places in London are associated with certain important institutions and are often used in the media and in general conversation to refer to those institutions. Put each one in its correct place in the sentences below.

Whitehall	**Fleet Street**	**Scotland Yard**	**Buckingham**
the City	**10 Downing**	**the West End**	**Palace**
the Old Bailey	**Street**	**Westminster**	

(a) His criminal career started with theft and pick-pocketing and ended up at _____ on a murder charge.

(b) Although he's only just entered Parliament, he's already aiming at _____.

(c) There are likely to be late nights and angry arguments at _____ when the new tax proposals are debated next week.

(d) _____ has denied reports that the Queen is shortly going to abdicate.

(e) After the prison escape, _____ alerted all police forces to be on the look-out for the man.

(f) He's an important man in _____. He's director of a big bank or insurance firm or something.

(g) She's a good actress but she won't really feel she's succeeded until she has a leading part in _____.

(h) There are rumours in _____ about the possible launching of a new newspaper next year.

(i) There have been growing complaints that bureaucracy in _____ is slowing down the enforcement of government legislation.

Places, people, institutions
Each group below contains the names of well-known British places, people or institutions. Find, in each group, the item which does not belong.

E.g. the Highlands
Snowdonia
the Pennines
the Channel
the Lake District

Answer: all are mountainous areas except the Channel, which is the sea between England and France

(a)	(b)	(c)
Kent	Thames	Man
Yorkshire	Severn	Ulster
Cornwall	Clyde	Jersey
Surrey	Windsor	Scilly
Manchester	Tyne	Wight

(d)	(e)	(f)
Thatcher	Wren	Graham Greene
Victoria	Wellington	George Orwell
Gladstone	Nelson	William Turner
Disraeli	Montgomery	Charles Dickens
Churchill	Drake	Somerset Maugham

(g)	(h)	(i)
Knightsbridge	Regents Street	Heathrow
Soho	the Cenotaph	Wembley
Brighton	Piccadilly	Crystal Palace
Chelsea	Oxford Street	Lords
Mayfair	the Mall	Wimbledon

(j) Green
Yellow
Labour
S.L.D.
Conservative

(k) Sainsburys
Marks & Spencer
Harrods
Boots
W.H. Smith

(l) Birmingham
Edinburgh
Belfast
Cardiff
London

(m) I.C.I.
British Leyland
British Aerospace
The British
   Council
Unilever

(n) Guardian
Times
Independent
Observer
Time

(o) public
primary
preparatory
comprehensive
gymnasium

(p) Midland
Lloyds
Barclays
National Trust
National
   Westminster

(q) Waterloo
Hampton Court
Victoria
King's Cross
Paddington

(r) Chequers
Pentonville
Wormwood
   Scrubs
Dartmoor
Holloway

(s) Buckingham
   Palace
Windsor
Balmoral
Kew Gardens
Sandringham

(t) Eton
Harrow
Oxford
Gordonstoun
Winchester

(u) the Grand
   National
Boxing Day
Test Matches
the Cup Final
the Boat Race

Key

The answers to some of the exercises in this book are a matter of opinion. In these cases, no answer is given here.

Topics

City Life (p.1)   a) city-dwellers b) irresistible lure c) metropolis d) cosmopolitan e) stimulation f) anonymity g) cost of living h) pollution i) urban j) to breed crime k) commuter l) congestion

Issues in Education (p.1)   a) classless b) streaming c) gifted d) potential e) elite f) privileged g) labelled h) inferiority complex i) divisive j) conventional k) spontaneity l) cram

Fashion in Clothes (p.2)   a) individualists b) slaves to fashion c) haute couture d) fashion houses e) trends f) trendy g) dictate h) the latest fashion i) personal ornaments j) slavishly k) dictates l) conformists

Compulsory Military Service (p.2)   a) conscription b) controversial c) discipline d) initiative e) conscripts f) amateur g) professional h) volunteers i) disruption j) pacifist k) conscientious objector l) voluntary

Advertising (p.3)   a) implicit b) subtle c) exploit d) ubiquitous e) catchy jingles f) bombard g) brainwash h) beneficial i) informative j) watchdog k) blatant l) misleading

How Much Freedom Should Children Have? (p.3)   a) permissive b) adolescence c) formative d) run wild e) juvenile delinquency f) authoritarian g) possessive h) rebelliousness i) suppress j) upbringing k) inhibited

Censorship (p.4)   a) excessive b) gratuitous c) corrupting d) masquerading e) unscrupulous f) perverted g) degrades h) banned i) counter-productive j) infringes k) moral standards l) safeguards

Love (p.4)   a) idolize b) hero-worship c) mature d) infatuation e) flirtation f) partners g) one-sided h) mutual i) platonic j) stable k) compatible l) complement

Attitudes to Work and Leisure (p.5)   a) aspire b) initiative c) constructively d) aimless e) fulfilment f) conditioned g) regimentation h) rewarding i) creativity j) 9 to 5 k) scope l) challenge

The Purpose of State Punishment (p.5)   a) reform b) rehabilitate c) deterrent d) retribution e) wrongdoer f) misdeeds g) crime doesn't pay h) corporal punishment i) death penalty j) barbaric k) humane l) law-abiding

Women's Rights (p.6)   a) feminist b) discrimination c) male chauvinist d) the weaker sex e) militant f) battle of the sexes g) sexist h) second-class citizens i) exploitation j) sex objects k) male-dominated l) unisex

Modern Values (p.6)   a) affluence b) materialistic c) acquisitive d) status e) image f) status-symbols g) welfare state h) idealism i) mercenary j) motivated k) priorities l) spiritual

Related Word Groups

Body (p.7)   a) jaw, lid, lash, pupil, temple, lobe, gums, nostril b) elbow, biceps, forearm, thumb, palm, wrist, fist, knuckles c) calf, thigh, shin, instep, heel, sole, toes, ankle

Books (p.7)   **1** a) manuscript b) proofs c) volume d) publication e) copy f) hardback, paperback g) best-seller h) edition i) thriller j) whodunnit **2** a) An encyclopaedia is usually in several volumes, while a dictionary is normally only one. b) A whodunnit (= who did it? i.e. Who was the murderer?) c) A thriller, because it is thrilling, exciting. d) From a government or similar publication. e) 'Have you got a copy of . . . ?' f) The author must hand in the manuscript. g) The proofs must be checked. h) Every author hopes for a best-seller. i) Buy paperbacks instead of hardbacks. **3** a) browse b) skip c) look up d) refer to e) read from cover to cover, dip into f) wade through g) peruse h) skim i) flip through **5** a) key b) acknowledgements c) 'blurb' d) glossary e) index f) dedication g) footnotes, appendix h) bibliography i) frontispiece j) contents k) chronology

Dirt and Damage (p.9)   **1** a) scratched b) faded c) shabby d) torn e) soiled f) smeared g) rusty h) stained i) shop-soiled j) smudged k) blunt l) filthy

Drinking (p.10)   **1** a) never drinks alcohol b) doesn't want other people to know he drinks c) only drinks with other people, e.g. at parties d) has a drink from time to time e) is addicted to alcohol f) is often drunk g) is a poor person, often homeless, who drinks anything, anywhere h) drinks a lot i) runs a pub j) serves people in a pub k) produces beer in large quantities **3** a) a non-alcoholic fruit drink b) a mixed alcoholic drink c) a last (alcoholic) drink before going to bed d) a last drink before driving e) a mixture of beer and lemonade (or a similar drink) f) a mixture of wine or spirits and hot water, sugar, lemon etc. g) a refreshing non-alcoholic drink, e.g. squash, Coca-Cola h) a single drink of spirits **5** a) corkscrew b) pub crawl, hangover c) vineyard d) toast e) sip f) cheers g) breathalyzer h) drop i) booze j) intoxicated k) stagger **7** a) 'sober' means 'not drunk' b) 'tipsy' means 'slightly drunk' c) 'fizzy' means 'effervescent' (with bubbles), 'still' means 'not fizzy' (especially soft drinks) d) 'draught beer' is served direct from the barrel or container, not in bottles e) you are 'teetotal' if you never drink alcohol but if you are 'on the wagon', you might only have stopped temporarily f) 'vintage wine' is a good wine of a certain age and maturity, 'plonk' is colloquial for cheap, ordinary wine g) you can drink in a 'pub', but an 'off-licence' is a shop selling alcohol to take away h) whisky is 'neat' when nothing else is added to the glass, 'on the rocks' means 'with ice' i) 'Dutch courage' is the confidence you get from a drink, e.g. whisky, but 'to go Dutch' means that each person pays for him or herself, e.g. in a pub

Driving (p.12)   **1** a) indicated b) accelerated c) overtook d) turned on e) dipped f) sounded g) swerved h) applied i) skidded j) reversed k) pulled up l) checked m) fastened n) adjusted o) started p) released

Food (p.12)   **1** a) peck at b) chew, swallow c) consume d) polish off e) gorge f) gnaw g) bolt, digest h) lick **3** a) pig b) cow c) pig d) deer e) calf f) sheep g) pig **4** a) a chicken b) a nut c) cheese d) dough e) an orange f) a rabbit g) a loaf h) a joint of meat **5** a) meat b) a hard-boiled egg c) a pancake d) cream e) a chicken f) potatoes g) eggs h) a cake **6** a) 'starving' means 'very hungry', 'parched' means 'very dry', 'very thirsty' b) a 'snack' is a very quick, light meal but 'a square meal' is a proper, substantial meal c) bread goes 'stale' after a few days and goes 'mouldy' after a few more days when a fungus begins to grow on it d) 'peckish' means 'rather hungry' but 'ravenous' means 'extremely hungry', 'starving' e) unattractive or badly-cooked food is 'uneatable', but food which is simply not suitable or possible for humans to eat is 'inedible' f) a 'beer-bottle' is a bottle intended to contain beer, possibly empty, but a 'bottle of beer' is a bottle with beer in it g) a 'starter' is a small dish before the main course of a meal, a 'dessert' (fruit, pudding) comes at the end h) a 'restaurant' serves complete lunches and dinners only, but a 'café' serves all meals and often simple snacks and drinks

Friends (p.14) **1** a) compatriot b) pen-pal c) companion d) partner e) mate f) bosom pal g) rival h) companion i) old flame j) mate k) foe l) colleague m) fair-weather friend n) confidant o) mate p) acquaintance q) associate

Light (p.15) **1** a) floodlight b) flare c) glow d) flash, lightning e) twinkle f) dazzle g) flicker h) spark i) sparkle **2** a) headlights b) traffic-lights c) torch d) son et lumière e) limelight f) footlights g) spotlight h) searchlight i) chandelier j) lantern

Materials (p.16) **1** a) comfortable soft trousers b) a ship's sail etc. c) jeans d) a woman's expensive, warm coat e) bathroom windows f) church windows g) the roof of a shed or cheap hut h) a man's old-fashioned light summer hat i) a wall j) cutlery **2** a) a wine-bottle stopper b) a woman's expensive evening dress c) shoes, a casual jacket d) fine bed-sheets e) an ordinary soldier's uniform f) packing material g) a man's hard-wearing sports-jacket h) fine cups etc. i) old ships j) a lawn

Memory (p.17) **1** a) haunt b) nostalgia c) lasting d) reminisce e) cast f) total recall g) sieve h) memorable i) blank j) absent-minded **2** a) I know it, but I can't quite remember. b) I tried very hard to remember or to think of an idea. c) Is this name familiar? d) I completely forgot it. e) She remembers every detail clearly. f) I have memorized it.

Money (p.17) **1** a) currency b) counterfeit c) numismatist d) counterfoil, expenditure e) bounce f) standing order g) statement h) legal tender **2** a) broke b) make ends meet c) chickenfeed d) quid e) mortgage f) I.O.U. g) hire purchase, instalments

Numbers (p.18) a) hat-trick b) scores c) cardinal, ordinal d) dozen e) gross f) Roman g) even, odd h) digits i) odd j) good k) average l) round

People (p.19) **1** a) a day-dreamer b) a busybody c) a dare-devil d) a rolling stone e) a sponger f) a battle-axe g) a golden boy h) a slow coach i) a crank j) a pain in the neck k) a lone wolf l) a tomboy **2** a) a wind-bag b) a miser c) a name-dropper d) a slave-driver e) a jay-walker f) a layabout g) a litter-lout h) a road-hog i) a clock-watcher j) a fare-dodger k) a slob l) a tear-away

Small Quantities (p.20) **1** a) speck b) crumb c) blade d) dot e) grain f) shred g) fragment h) glimmer i) grain j) trace k) trace **2** a) drop b) clue c) breath d) drop e) dash f) hint g) scrap h) puff i) scrap j) item k) flake

Social Types (p.21) **1** a) life and soul of the party b) wet blanket c) good mixer d) gate-crasher e) wallflower f) chatterbox g) gossip h) femme fatale i) Don Juan j) social climber **3** a) good company b) snob c) killjoy d) early bird e) loner f) bore g) jet-setter h) parasite i) socialite j) trouble-maker

Sounds (p.22) **1** a) scream b) moan c) cheer d) boo e) chant f) gasp g) snort h) drone i) whimper j) yell **3** a) toll b) chime c) tinkle d) thud e) sizzle f) blare g) hiss

h) swish i) clink j) pop **5** a) squelch b) plop c) rattle d) boom e) chirrup f) squeak g) rumble h) click i) hoot j) murmur **7** a) large bell b) clock c) violin-string breaking d) iron gates closing e) car horn f) electronic personal caller g) gun h) light rain on window i) wood fire burning j) car braking at speed k) horses' hoofs on road l) bath-water going down plug-hole m) spoon tapping empty glass

Space Travel (p.24) a) gravity b) manned c) astronaut d) launching pad e) launch f) countdown g) lift-off h) splashdown i) spacecraft j) orbit k) dock l) mission

Sport (p.25) **1** a) a pitch b) a pool c) a course d) a track e) a court f) a court g) a court h) a ring i) a range j) a rink k) a circuit l) a track/course **2** a) puck/stick b) bow/arrows c) club/tee d) racket/net e) racket/shuttlecock f) gloves/gumshield g) helmet/steering-wheel h) whip/reins i) saddle/handlebars j) rifle/target k) toboggan/goggles l) parallel bars/mat m) épée/mask **3** a) horse-racing ('The race has begun!') b) boxing ('Assistants out of the ring!') c) golf ('Get out of the way of the ball!') d) football ('Referee, someone's broken the rules!') e) tennis, table-tennis ('The score is forty points to zero.') f) athletics ('Get ready to start the race.') g) football etc. ('The score is three goals to zero.') h) archery, shooting ('Right in the middle of the target!') i) show-jumping ('The rider has lost four penalty points.')

Time (p.26) **1** a) the small hours b) digital c) local time d) time zones e) chronological f) decade, century g) spell h) era i) turn of the century **2** a) Dawn is the first light of day and dusk is the last b) a month can be any period of 28 days, but a calendar month specifies that one of the 12 named months of the year, e.g. April, is meant c) a leap year is one in which February has 29 days

Tools and Equipment (p.26) **1** a) a stethoscope b) a rake c) a whip d) a rolling pin e) a hose f) an axe g) a baton h) an anvil i) a plane j) an exposure meter k) a spanner l) an anchor **2** a) a bow b) a bucket c) a net d) a tape measure e) a scalpel f) a torch g) a truncheon h) a trowel i) a drier j) a spade k) a pneumatic drill l) a compass **3** a) a turntable b) flippers c) a briefcase d) a catalogue e) a vacuum cleaner f) radar g) scaffolding h) a parking meter i) a hearse j) blueprints k) a palette l) a crane **4** a) a score b) a sniffer dog c) a loom d) a whistle e) a last f) headphones g) a plough h) a kiln i) a filing cabinet j) a clapperboard k) a drill l) a till

Water (p.28) **1** a) source, estuary b) current c) ebb and flow, tide d) tributary e) river bed, river bank f) lock **2** a) mixture of rain and snow b) light fog at seashore or on river c) continuous light rain d) mixture of smoke and fog e) frozen rain falling as bits of ice f) moisture found on grass at dawn **3** a) trickle b) spill c) squirt d) irrigate e) water f) drip g) splash h) pour i) dribble j) soak k) flow, meander

Word Formation

Word Forms (p.29) **1** a) beautiful b) beautician c) beautify **2** a) payment b) payable c) payee **3** a) receptionist b) receipt c) receptive **4** a) heroism b) heroically c) heroine **5** a) production b) producers c) unproductive **6** a) explanatory b) inexplicable c) explanation **7** a) incomparably, comparison b) comparative **8** a) inadvisable b) advisory

c) advisability **9** a) admirers b) admiration c) admirable **10** a) stabilize b) instability c) unstable **11** a) economize b) uneconomical c) economic **12** a) residence b) residential c) residents **13** a) comforting b) uncomfortable c) discomfort **14** a) deaths b) deadly c) deaden **15** a) demonstrators b) undemonstrative c) demonstrably **16** a) imitation b) imitative c) inimitable **17** a) argument b) argumentative c) arguably **18** a) unrepeatable b) repetitive c) repetition **19** a) unfailingly b) failure c) failing **20** a) discourage b) courageously c) encouragement **21** a) unrealistic b) reality c) realist **22** a) falsifying b) falsehood c) falsity **23** a) prophet, prophecy b) prophetic **24** a) indescribable b) descriptive c) description **25** a) friendship b) befriended c) unfriendly **26** a) sensation b) insensitive c) senseless **27** a) fame b) infamous, infamy **28** a) defensive b) indefensible c) defence **29** a) disagreeable b) agreement c) agreeable **30** a) possessions b) possessive c) possessor **31** a) differ b) differentiate c) differences **32** a) activists b) activated c) inactive **33** a) formative b) deformity c) formation **34** a) compulsory b) compulsion c) compelling **35** a) enthusiastically b) enthusiast c) enthuse **36** a) creator b) creative c) creation **37** a) necessitate b) necessarily c) necessities **38** a) indestructible b) destruction c) destructive **39** a) management b) unmanageable c) managerial/management **40** a) unbelievable b) beliefs c) disbelief

Portmanteau Words (p.33) a) Eurovision (Europe + television) b) Oxfam (Oxford + famine) c) Interpol (International + Police) d) brunch (breakfast + lunch) e) Chunnel (Channel + tunnel) f) motel (motor + hotel) g) Oxbridge (Oxford + Cambridge) h) Swatch (Swiss + watch) i) bedsit (bedroom + sitting room)

Prefixes (p.34) **1** a) pseudo b) out c) arch d) mal e) arch f) out g) mal h) pseudo i) mal j) out **2** a) name under which an author writes instead of his or her real name b) fiercest rivals c) bad, inefficient administration d) extra-large sized clothes e) poor, insufficient nutrition f) falsely pretending to be religious g) a principal, especially bad villain h) to stay longer than your host wishes you to stay **3** a) neo b) fore c) a d) hyper e) neo f) hyper g) a h) fore i) fore j) hyper **4** a) a modern form of imperialism b) a person who believes there is no God c) an indication of what is to happen in the future d) an extremely large supermarket e) very high blood pressure f) a conclusion which was known or expected before g) not symmetric, irregular h) someone who believes in the old Fascist ideas **5** uniform, decade, century, quadrangle, monocle, tricycle, bicycle, bipeds, quadrupeds, binoculars, tripod, octopus, monorail, sextet, quintet, quartet, trio, bigamy, bilingual, pentathlon, septuagenarian, duologue, monologues, nonagenarian, centenarian, octogenarian, triplets **6** a) 200th anniversary of an event b) five-sided figure c) 100th anniversary of an event d) flag with three coloured stripes e) uninteresting, without change f) athletics contest in which each competitor takes part in ten events g) someone between 59 and 70 years old h) five children from one birth i) cut or divide into two parts j) one hundredth of a dollar k) aircraft with two pairs of wings l) parliament with two chambers m) cycle designed with one wheel n) four children from one birth o) mythical animal with one horn

Suffixes (p.36) **1** a) cide b) phobia c) gamy d) phobia e) cide f) gamy g) phobia h) cide **2** a) a solution or powder which kills germs b) fear or hatred of foreigners c) killing one's own father d) a society where it is the custom for a person to have a number of wives or husbands e) killing one's own brother f) fear of open spaces **3** a) monger b) phile c) monger d) maniac e) phile f) monger g) maniac h) maniac **4** a) someone obsessed with setting fire to property b) a love of France and French culture c) someone who sells fish from a shop d) someone who loves England and English culture e) an obsession f) someone who is obsessed with films **5** a) like b) most c) worthy d) like e) like f) worthy g) most h) worthy **6** a) a practical, efficient manner b) his main thought, the one at the very front of his mind c) a car that is fit for use on the road d) a comment worth making a note of and remembering e) a statue which looks almost alive f) the defences furthest out from the centre **7** a) some b) wards c) esque d) wards e) some f) wards g) some h) esque **8** a) boys who are always quarrelling b) apparently confident c) a figure as striking and impressive as a statue d) a movement towards the ground e) a person who makes you tired and irritated f) a novel in the style of the writer, Kafka **9** a) scope b) let c) scape d) ling e) ette f) scape g) let h) scope i) scape **10** a) an insect so small it can only be seen properly through a microscope b) a small, young pig c) a small, young duck d) a small kitchen e) a marvellous cloud formation f) a small book **11** a) is interested in birds. b) is interested in stamps. c) believes in equal rights for women. d) is interested in coins. e) gives large amounts of money to charity. f) performs post-mortems on dead bodies. g) speaks many languages. h) writes plays. i) is an expert on earthquakes. j) looks after people's hands and fingernails. k) makes up medicines. l) studies the weather. m) sets fire to property. n) stuffs dead animals. o) hates women. p) walks in his or her sleep. q) is an expert on China. r) looks after people's feet. s) is a handwriting expert.

Compound Adjectives (p.39) **1** a) That's a dangerous-looking thing. b) Mr Reed is a London-born accountant. c) She is always very smartly-dressed. d) It was painted a brick-red colour. e) She had cat-like eyes. f) It was a happy-sad occasion. g) The tower is mushroom-shaped. h) He was world-famous. i) We had to write a 200-word composition. **2** a) It was an awful-tasting meal. b) Only single-engine/single-engined planes can land here. c) A five-storey building suddenly collapsed. d) We walked along a red-carpeted corridor. e) This machine is hand-operated. f) The new director is an Oxford-educated economist. g) He is very broad-shouldered. h) She's always very self-satisfied. i) My sister is very dress-conscious. **3** a) We'll have a French-speaking guide. b) The walls were sky-blue. c) I looked at the sea, which was blue-green. d) The ship sailed with an eight-man crew. e) She was fair-haired. f) The new, American-built, machinery will arrive next month. g) I heard a strange-sounding voice. h) These are man-eating tigers. i) He is always bad-tempered. **4** a) The experiment was done with gas-filled balloons. b) My teenage son is football-mad. c) I'm afraid my wife is very free-spending. d) He is certainly well-intentioned. e) They are very bad-mannered. f) The firm is New York-based. g) Those cars are very high-priced. h) The noise was ear-splitting! i) I need a four-door car.

Noun Plurals (p.40) **1** a) mice, geese, feet b) companies, stories, delays, deliveries, keys, ways c) chiefs, thieves, roofs, knives, safes d) photos, studios, Echoes, heroes e) passers-by, commanders-in-chief, brief-cases, police-cars, courts-martial/court-martials f) deer, sheep, aircraft **2** a) crises b) chateaux

c) memoranda d) analyses e) bureaux f) strata g) theses h) phenomena i) criteria j) media

Problem Words

Confusing Word Pairs (p.41) **1** a) disused b) misused c) misused d) disused **2** a) illegible b) unreadable c) illegible d) unreadable **3** a) dependent b) dependant c) dependant d) dependent **4** a) storey b) story c) story d) storey **5** a) historical b) historic c) historical d) historic **6** a) immigration b) emigration **7** a) draught b) draft c) draught d) draft **8** a) unsatisfied b) dissatisfied c) dissatisfied d) unsatisfied **9** a) suit b) suite c) suite d) suit **10** a) license c) license. d) licence **11** a) prophesy b) prophecy **12** a) devise b) device c) device d) devise **13** a) goal b) gaol c) goal d) gaol **14** a) enquiries b) inquiries c) enquiries d) inquiry **15** a) exhaustive b) exhausting c) exhausting d) exhaustive **16** a) uninterested b) disinterested c) uninterested d) disinterested **17** a) counsel b) council c) counsel d) council **18** a) counsellor b) councillor **19** a) unknown b) infamous c) infamous d) unknown **20** a) Surely b) certainly c) surely d) certainly **21** a) diary b) dairy c) dairy d) diary **22** a) complement b) compliment c) compliment d) complement **23** a) First b) at first c) At first d) First **24** a) at last b) lastly c) At last d) lastly
Difficult Verb Pairs (p.45) **1** a) fallen b) felled c) fell **2** a) founded b) found c) founded **3** a) bounded b) bounded c) bound **4** a) saw b) sawed c) sawed **5** a) grounded b) ground c) ground **6** a) wound b) wounded c) wind **7** a) laid b) lay c) laid d) lie e) lay f) lie **8** a) born b) borne c) borne **9** a) laden b) loaded c) laden **10** a) costed b) cost c) costed **11** a) hung b) hanged c) hung **12** a) stricken b) struck c) stricken
Ambiguous Words (p.47) a) correct/not left b) with light skin or hair/reasonable c) amusing/strange. peculiar d) without work to do/lazy e) know who he was/accept him as President f) inquisitive/strange. peculiar g) inexpensive/poor quality h) due, scheduled/obliged, had to i) physically strong/influential j) felt suspicion/caused others to suspect him k) envious/protective l) invite to her home for dinner-party etc./amuse with jokes etc. m) probably will/ought to, has an obligation to n) ask me for help/I didn't like him o) well-liked/aimed at a wide circulation, non-intellectual p) perhaps he phoned/I'm annoyed he didn't phone q) ready/willing r) said they definitely did it/made them do and accepted no excuses s) exploited unfairly/took benefit from. put into use
False Friends (p.48) **1** a) present b) actual c) present **2** a) ignore b) not know c) ignore **3** a) wonderful b) formidable c) formidable d) wonderful **4** a) camping b) camp-site **5** a) morale b) moral c) moral d) morale **6** a) attend b) frequent c) frequent d) attend **7** a) adequate b) suitable c) suitable d) adequate **8** a) subject b) argument c) argument d) subject **9** a) possibly b) eventually c) possibly d) eventually **10** a) dancing b) dance-hall **11** a) experience b) experiment c) experience d) experiment **12** a) fabricate b) manufacture c) fabricate d) manufacture **13** a) driver b) chauffeur c) chauffeur d) driver **14** a) attend b) assist c) attend d) assist **15** a) pass b) take c) take. pass **16** a) remark b) notice c) notice d) remark **17** a) souvenir b) memory c) souvenir d) memory **18** a) stamp b) print

c) print d) stamp **19** a) meeting b) reunion c) meeting. reunion **20** a) nice b) sympathetic c) nice d) sympathetic **21** a) corpse b) Corps c) Corps d) corpse **22** a) voyage b) journey c) journey d) voyage **23** a) legend b) key c) key d) legend **24** a) obtain b) become c) become d) obtain **25** a) On the contrary b) on the other hand c) on the other hand d) On the contrary **26** a) review b) critic c) critic, review

Idiom

Alliterative Expressions (p.53) **1** a) rat race b) brickbats c) chit-chat d) ship-shape e) mish-mash f) wishy-washy **2** a) dilly-dally b) zigzag c) sob-story d) creepy-crawly e) sing-song f) Flip-flops **3** a) shilly-shally b) hot-head c) tittle-tattle d) riff-raff e) tell-tale f) topsy-turvy

Animals (p.54) **1** a) bookworm b) dog-collar c) puppy fat d) crocodile tears e) wolf-whistles f) zebra crossing g) stag party h) dark horse i) wild-goose chase **2** a) dog-eared b) fly on the wall c) bird's-eye view d) donkey's years e) parrot-fashion f) cat's eyes g) guinea pig h) frog in my throat i) pigeon-holes **3** a) ram b) monkey c) badgered d) hounded e) ducked f) worm g) fox h) dogged

Body (p.55) **1** a) brave, resolute b) mean, not generous c) generous d) businesslike. unemotional e) conceited. self-important f) cowardly, nervous g) dishonest, liable to steal h) silent, unwilling to speak i) hypocritical j) over-romantic k) insensitive to criticism **2** a) head b) shoulder c) elbow d) thumb e) finger f) foot g) mouth h) shin i) head j) back

Collocations (p.56) **1** a) bone b) dirt c) dog d) stone e) brand f) wide g) stark h) pitch **2** a) razor b) fast c) crystal d) bone e) flat f) blind g) paper h) wide **3** a) bitter b) thin c) dire d) blank e) broad f) all-out g) rock h) blind

Colour (p.57) **1** a) in black and white b) to catch someone red-handed c) a Black Maria d) red tape e) to have green fingers f) a black sheep g) green with envy h) once in a blue moon i) in the red j) out of the blue **2** a) a blackleg b) a white-collar job c) a green belt d) to see red e) a white lie f) a white elephant g) rose-coloured spectacles h) a red-letter day i) a red herring j) to give the green light to

'Do' and 'Make' (p.58) **1** a) do b) do. make c) make d) make e) make. make f) make g) do. make h) make i) Do. make j) do **2** a) make, do b) make c) make d) do, make e) do f) make. make g) make h) make. do i) do j) make **3** a) make. make b) do c) Make d) do e) do. make f) make. make g) do. make h) make i) make j) do

Fictional Characters in Everyday Language (p.59) **1** a) James Bond (daring intelligence agent in novels by Ian Fleming) b) Billy Bunter (fat schoolboy, always eating, in stories by Frank Richards) c) Peter Pan (boy who never grows up in play by J.M. Barrie) d) Robinson Crusoe (man who finds himself alone on a remote desert island in novel by Daniel Defoe) e) Scrooge (very mean character in *Christmas Carol* by Charles Dickens) f) Man Friday (all-purpose servant of Robinson Crusoe) g) Superman (character who can achieve miracles. from American comic strip) h) Robin Hood (legendary outlaw who 'robbed the rich to feed the poor') i) Sherlock Holmes (brilliant. shrewd private detective in novels by Conan Doyle) **2** a) Jekyll and

Hyde (man with two contrasting personalities, one gentle and one murderous, in novel by R.L. Stevenson) b) Old Uncle Tom Cobbleigh and all (i.e. 'everyone', characters in traditional folk song 'Widdicombe Fair') c) Big Brother (sinister dictator figure in totalitarian state in George Orwell's novel *1984*) d) Little Lord Fauntleroy (very elegantly-dressed little boy in novel by F.H. Burnett) e) Cinderella (girl in fairy-tale who is treated as a slave by her family) f) Tarzan (strong, muscular hero of stories of Edgar Rice Burroughs) g) Walter Mitty (man who constantly escaped from reality into heroic day-dreams in James Thurber's *The Secret Life of Walter Mitty*) h) Rip Van Winkle (man who slept for 20 years in story by Washington Irving)

Food (p.60) **1** a) a butter-fingers b) in a jam c) money for jam d) a vegetable e) peanuts f) the cream g) the salt of the earth h) full of beans i) sour grapes j) nuts k) cup of tea l) a piece of cake **2** a) cucumber b) beetroot c) toast d) pancake e) mustard f) chalk and cheese g) hot cakes h) sardines i) jelly j) water

'Hand' (p.61) **1** a) offhand b) underhand c) cap in hand d) out of hand e) hand-to-mouth f) to hand **2** a) offhand b) in good hands c) empty-handed d) high-handed e) short-handed f) single-handed **3** a) to give him a free hand b) to keep his hand in c) to wash his hands of d) to have the upper hand e) to win hands down f) to have a hand in

Letter-Words and Phrases (p.62) **1** a) T-junction b) A-bomb c) T-shirt d) S-bend e) U-turn f) L-plates g) X-ray h) V-formation i) V-neck **2** a) have to be careful of his behaviour b) a street-atlas of the town c) don't pronounce the 'h' at the beginning of a word d) reading (w)riting and (a)rithmetic (conventional foundation of elementary education)

Names (p.62) **1** a) bobby b) Jack of all trades c) peeping Tom d) smart Alec e) Tom, Dick or Harry f) doubting Thomas **2** a) I don't know him from Adam b) keeping up with the Joneses c) before you could say Jack Robinson d) robbing Peter to pay Paul

Numbers (p.63) **1** a) nine-day wonder b) two-edged compliment c) one-armed bandit d) one-track mind e) four-letter word f) one-man band g) three-cornered contest **2** a) the third degree b) sixth sense c) on first-name terms d) in her seventh heaven e) to play second fiddle f) third-rate g) to have second thoughts h) at the eleventh hour

Pairs (p.64) **1** a) collar and tie b) prim and proper c) song and dance d) by and large e) chop and change f) tooth and nail g) hard and fast h) length and breadth i) cloak and dagger j) pins and needles **2** a) sick and tired b) spick and span c) odds and ends d) ups and downs e) down and out f) pros and cons g) up and about h) safe and sound i) to and fro j) ins and outs

Phrasal Verbs (p.65) **1** a) see off b) take down c) try out d) bring up e) get down f) call off g) bring up h) put up **2** a) let down b) make up c) bear out d) put off e) leave out f) run down g) put forward h) rule out **3** a) pull down, put up b) give away c) turn out d) look up e) turn away f) do up g) put off **4** a) stand for b) account for c) get over d) run into e) get round f) take to g) come into h) take after **5** a) go back on b) be up to c) catch up with d) put up with e) make up for f) do away with g) be up to h) look down on **6** a) turn in b) turn up c) fall through d) break out e) look up f) go off g) break up h) come out **7** a) fall off b) come up c) go down d) break down e) fall out f) hold on g) Drop in h) drop off

Rhyming Expressions (p.67) **1** a) big-wigs b) prime-time c) nitty-gritty d) go-slow e) higgledy-piggledy f) humdrum g) pell-mell h) brain-drain **2** a) walkie-talkie b) fun-run c) roly-poly d) silly-billy e) space-race f) mumbo-jumbo g) willy-nilly h) hanky-panky **3** a) meals-on-wheels b) make or break c) la-di-da d) wear and tear e) wine and dine f) moan and groan

'Say' and 'Tell' (p.68) a) tell b) said c) say d) say e) tell f) say g) say h) telling i) say j) saying k) tell l) say m) say n) say o) tell p) say q) tell

Status (p.69) a) would-be b) late c) The headmaster present d) ex- e) The present headmaster f) sacked g) actual h) stop-gap i) in question j) -to-be k) so-called

Time (p.69) **1** a) At one time b) At the time c) at times d) for the time being e) on time f) in time **2** a) in his time b) behind the times c) at the same time d) pressed for time e) before my time f) in no time **3** a) in the nick of time b) All in good time c) for old time's sake d) About time too e) time on his hands f) time after time **4** a) take his time b) keep up with the times c) kill time d) make time e) bide his time

Identification

Objects (p.71) a) bicycle b) briefcase c) television set d) book e) piano f) watch g) tree h) pistol, revolver i) map

Newspaper Parts (p.72) a) weather forecast b) gossip column c) caption d) headline e) obituary f) horoscope g) editorial h) recipe i) auction report j) court circular k) football l) travel and holidays m) crossword clues n) parliamentary report o) gardening tips p) readers' advice column q) television preview r) new car report

The Arts (p.73) a) classical music concert b) exhibition of paintings c) novel d) dance, ballet e) play, theatrical performance f) photographs g) film

Occupations (p.74) a) mens' tailor b) supermarket cashier c) airline pilot d) gardener e) hospital nurse f) taxi-driver g) priest, vicar h) fireman i) cinema usherette j) newspaper reporter

Occasions (p.75) a) terrorist bomb explosion b) circus c) political, diplomatic meeting d) factory strike e) trial in court f) street demonstration g) parliamentary election

Descriptions

Diagrams (p. 76)

a)

b)

c)

d)

Plans (p. 78)

a)

b)

c)

d)

Maps (p. 80)

a)

b)

People's Appearance (p.82) **1** a) lanky b) bowler hat c) double-breasted d) bow-tie e) cuff f) creases g) button-hole h) tucked i) breast pocket j) formally **2** a) skinny b) grin c) patched d) slanting e) lapels f) plain g) pigeon-toed h) casually i) bare-footed j) trainers **3** a) strongly-built b) broad c) waist d) clean-shaven e) bare-headed f) closely-cropped g) expression h) buckle i) upright j) hips **4** a) teens b) slender c) figure d) clasped e) wavy f) parted g) bow h) pleated i) polo-neck j) high-heeled **5** a) thirtyish b) folded c) bow-legged d) obese e) flat cap f) side-burns g) checked h) rolled up i) baggy j) braces

Style

Newspaper Headlines (p.84) **1** a) POLLS RIGGED b) GEMS HAUL c) TWO SOUGHT d) SERVICE CHIEFS e) CABINET RESHUFFLE **2** a) GEMS b) HAUL c) RIG d) CHIEF e) SWOOP f) SEEK/SOUGHT g) GAG h) DRAMA i) POLL(S) j) RESHUFFLE k) QUIT **4** a) FOIL b) PLEA c) BID d) HALT e) BAN f) CLASH g) BACK h) OUST i) FLEE j) WOO k) MOVE l) QUIZ **5** a) RIDDLE b) LEAK c) ENVOY d) AXE e) LIFT f) RAP g) BAFFLED h) CURB i) SPLIT j) PROBE k) CALL l) STORM

Formal English (p.86) **1** (other versions possible) a) This information may be changed. b) Look on the other side for more information. c) You must keep it and show it if you're asked to. d) If you're a married woman, write your surname when you were single. e) You must give this part of the ticket to the usherette. f) Fill in the part at the bottom. Then tear it off. g) Stick a recent photograph of yourself here. h) The information may be changed without warning. i) Look at the notes on the other side. j) Put the right amount of money in. The machine doesn't give change. k) If you don't order quickly, they may have run out of what you want. l) Trains printed in very black letters or numbers only have sleeping cars, no ordinary carriages. m) Cross out whatever doesn't apply to you. n) Ask inside. o) Reduced prices if you go in a group. p) You can't use it for the underground, except for certain trains. q) Put a tick in the right box according to whether you're married, single, divorced, widowed etc. r) You must pay a deposit when you book, and you won't get it back. s) The date when the ticket is no good any more. t) Write the complete name of your wife or husband. u) There's no need to tip anyone. v) Please don't smoke. w) They can refuse to let anyone in if they want to. x) On top of the price you must pay VAT (Value Added Tax). y) If you smoke, sit at the back. **2** (other versions possible) a) If there's anything wrong with the machine, go back to the shop where you got it. b) Do what it says on the other side. c) The firm doesn't take responsibility for anything which goes wrong if it isn't their fault. d) You won't necessarily be given a place just because you've got their minimum requirements. e) If you decide you want to keep the car longer than you originally agreed, it's important to tell the firm immediately. f) They don't promise to deliver the mail to the actual person whose name is on the address, only to the address itself. Whoever takes it from the postman will sign for it. g) Normally you've got to tell the bank seven days before you want to take any money out of a Deposit Account, but if it's an emergency you can get it immediately. h) You'll get four tickets, but if you want extra books you can get more tickets just by asking for them. i) It's not absolutely necessary to have this letter, but if you do have it, it'll make it much easier to get into the country. j) For the first 12 months after you arrive you can drive on an up-to-date International Driving Permit or driving licence from your own country, which you must have with you. Otherwise you must get a British driving licence. k) If you have an accident, you must pay the first £45 of any damage caused, but if you pay an extra 95p a day, you won't have to pay anything. l) You don't have to pay for a collect call, even if the person you want to call doesn't agree to pay. If that person doesn't agree to pay, then you can pay. If neither of you agrees to pay, you won't get your call. **3** (other versions possible) a) Any complaints should be addressed to the tour operator. b) We regret that no refunds can be made on sale purchases. c) Children will be admitted without charge if accompanied by an adult. d) In the event of fire please leave in an orderly fashion by the exits marked on the plan below. e) Travellers are advised to contact their embassy in the event of any problems which may occur. f) Patrons are requested to refrain from smoking. g) Please note that you should be in possession of a valid visa, which may be obtained from the consulate. h) A Certificate of Posting may be obtained at the time of posting (to be completed by the counter clerk) or later. on payment of a higher fee. i) See page 14 for further information. j) Valid for all trains departing after 7 p.m. k) Subject to alteration, especially in adverse weather conditions. l) This receipt to be retained and produced on request. m) Goods will not be dispatched until receipt of full remittance. n) Please enquire at reception about our sports facilities. o) A Certificate of Attendance will be given on production of an Admission Slip. A note from your teacher confirming your regular attendance is not obligatory but will greatly facilitate matters.

Colloquial English and Slang (p.89) **1** a) me b) pounds c) without money d) five-pound note e) wonderful f) thanks **2** a) thing that I can't remember the name of b) person whose name I've forgotten **3** a) all right b) children c) pleasant d) group e) marvellous f) man **4** a) don't like very much b) man c) yes d) conceited person e) uses his position unfairly f) trouble g) be serious h) courage i) be dismissed **5** a) high-class b) a celebration c) at my expense d) moment e) drunk **6** a) depressed b) what's wrong? c) stolen d) umbrella e) hard luck **7** a) man b) falls in love with c) sad, sentimental film d) unoriginal e) approaching **8** a) dilapidated car b) worn out c) too old to be of any more use d) like e) high-class, grand f) lot of money **9** a) stolen b) spectacles. glasses c) stupid, silly d) mad, insane **10** a) useless person b) fashionable c) someone or something very special d) slow to understand, unintelligent e) has a high opinion of herself f) snobbish, supercilious g) dismiss her h) extremely upset

English in Advertising (p.91) **Trade Names 1** a) snack bar b) shoe-shop c) dry cleaners d) photo-processing shop e) photo-copying firm f) women's clothes shop g) children's clothes shop h) taxi firm i) dry cleaners j) snack bar k) garage and repair shop l) hairdressers m) travel agency n) car-hire firm **2** a) cleaning fluids b) pet food c) telephone answering machines d) strong glue e) beds f) rucksacks g) bathroom equipment h) video and audio home entry system **3** a) translating b) car repairs c) driving school d) security services e) accommodation f) health and slimming studio g) travel agency h) computer services **Puns** a) 'Pounds' refers first to money and second to weight. b) They go up literally but also raise their economic and perhaps social level. c) 'Sound' refers to the quality of musical reproduction but also means 'good', 'reliable'. d) 'A good deal' can mean 'a lot' or 'a good business transaction'. e) 'Sleep on it' can also mean 'think about it'. f) 'Dying for' can also mean 'wanting desperately'. g) Figuratively this means 'you'll find your opinions expressed in the *Mirror* newspaper'. h) 'Snap' means 'immediate' or 'photograph'. i) The phrase means 'money topics' or 'money is important'. j) 'Naturally' means 'of course' or 'in a natural way'. k) 'Plane' has the same pronunciation as 'plain', meaning 'simple'. l) 'Red-carpet treatment' can mean

'special service and welcome'. m) 'Sea' is pronounced like 'see'. n) 'Stick using our glue' or 'remain our loyal customers'. o) 'Ties' can also mean 'connections' and 'loyalties'. p) 'Scents' is pronounced like 'sense'.
q) Figuratively an 'Indian Summer' is a pleasant, mild autumn. r) 'Food for thought' can mean 'something worth thinking about'.

Spoken English

Forms of Spoken Address (p.93) a) mum, mummy b) caller, nothing c) viewers d) grandad, grandpa e) nothing f) ladies and gentlemen g) sir h) Your Majesty i) nothing j) darling, love, dear k) listeners l) mate m) sir n) madam o) officer, nothing p) grandma, grannie q) dear, love r) sir s) men t) dad, daddy u) nothing
Colloquial Responses (p.94) **1** a) My lips are sealed. b) Dump it anywhere. c) The more the merrier. d) Flattery will get you nowhere. e) Care for a spin? **2** a) A little bird told me. b) I'm having second thoughts. c) Well, boys will be boys. d) Beggars can't be choosers. e) Well, you can't win them all. **3** a) Let's toss for it. b) OK. You toss, I'll call. Tails! c) I'm afraid I haven't a clue. d) Let me sleep on it. e) Oh, it's on the tip of my tongue. f) Cheers! g) Help yourself. c) No, it's my round. d) I could do with one. e) Oh, this is on me. **5** a) Be my guest. b) Back to square one. c) Yes, by the skin of my teeth. d) If you don't mind taking pot luck. e) Every little helps. **6** a) I'm all ears. b) I'm keeping my fingers crossed. c) It takes all sorts. d) Well, it can't be helped. e) OK. Thanks all the same. **7** a) You must be joking. b) Serves you right. c) Mind your own business. d) OK. Suit yourself. e) That'll be the day. **8** a) I can't be bothered. b) Have it your own way. c) How should I know? d) I like that! e) Rather you than me. **9** a) Stop preaching. b) I couldn't care less. c) Now you're talking. d) Yes, thanks to you. e) I don't get it.
Exclamations (p.96) **1** a) sh! b) eh? c) giddyup! d) there, there e) boo! f) whoops! g) well? h) wow! i) whoah! j) mm! **2** a) ta b) er c) now, now d) cheers! e) ta-ta f) hear, hear g) hi! h) oi! i) tut-tut j) gosh!
Spoken Numbers and Measurements (p.97) **1** a) 40 − 15 + 6 = 31 b) 81 ÷ 3 = 27 c) 3 × 6 = 18 d) Queen Elizabeth I reigned from 1558 to 1603. e) . . . at 7.30 p.m. on 2nd August. f) . . . £6.75. g) . . . on 411 4850. h) . . . is 44-7/509. i) . . . estimated at £2,471,850. j) The mixture is ²⁄₃ water. k) 1 litre = 1.76 pints. l) 22°₀ of the . . . m) . . . was 30 C, ie 86 F. n) . . . 4'2³₄" × 2'8'₁₂". o) . . . 3:0. p) . . . 3:3. q) . . . 30:0 to Becker. **2** a) Seventy-three plus twenty minus forty-three is fifty. b) One hundred and twenty-nine divided by three is forty-three. c) Four times twenty-one is eighty-four. d) Edward the Seventh died in nineteen ten. e) It was exactly eleven thirty-five a.m. on the twenty-first of May. f) . . . three pounds twenty-five pence each. g) . . . three oh seven double-two oh one. h) . . . eight stroke two dash double-seven one. i) . . . three million, two hundred and fifty-five thousand, eight hundred and forty. j) I am one eighth French. k) One mile is one point six oh nine kilometres. l) It is seventeen point three eight per cent gold. m) . . . thirty-two degrees fahrenheit, that is zero degrees centigrade. n) . . . two feet six and a half inches by five feet eight and a quarter inches. o) . . . three nil. p) . . . two all. q) . . . fifteen love . . .

Well-Known Spoken Phrases (p.98) a) Underground station announcer to passengers or lift attendant. b) Assistant in fast-food shop to customers. c) Friends or relatives wishing someone happy birthday. d) Court official asking accused person at beginning of trial whether he pleads guilty or not guilty. e) Customer asking hairdresser not to cut too much off. f) Customs officer to travellers passing through customs. g) Owner to dog telling it to keep close behind him. h) Doctor to patient telling him to get medicine from chemist's. i) Operator connecting caller. j) Customer asking for beer in a pub. k) Auctioneer when the bidding seems to have stopped. l) Someone announcing a toast to a newly-married couple. m) Priest at wedding ceremony. n) Witness in court. o) Dentist reassuring patient. p) Someone launching ship. q) Someone at the end of a prayer. r) Someone beginning a fairy-story. s) Photographer asking subject to smile. t) Crew member telling everyone to get on ship. u) Someone shouting that someone has fallen from ship.

Miscellaneous

Geo-political Names (p.99) **1** a) England is only one part of GB. b) GB includes England, Scotland and Wales. UK comprises GB and Northern Ireland. c) British Isles includes GB, all Ireland and all other islands in the area. d) 'Continental Europe' normally refers to mainland Europe, especially central and south. e) The Middle East is roughly between Egypt and Iran. The Far East is China, Korea, Japan etc. f) The subcontinent includes India, Pakistan, Bangladesh etc. g) America means US. North America also includes Canada and, technically, Mexico. h) South America is the land mass south of Panama. Latin America also includes Central America and Mexico. i) Arctic is north polar region. Antarctic south. j) Australasia includes Australia, New Zealand and other islands in the area. k) Southern Africa includes South Africa and neighbouring countries. **2** a) Arabic is normally only the language. b) Scotch normally refers only to products of Scotland, eg whisky, beef. c) Oriental = Eastern, Occidental = Western. **3** a) The Netherlands b) Persia c) The Federal Republic of Germany d) The German Democratic Republic e) Ceylon f) Eire g) Ulster **4** a) European Economic Community countries (most of W. Europe) b) Most countries of old British Empire (Canada, India, Australia etc.) c) North Atlantic Treaty Organization (US, Canada, most of W.Europe, Greece, Turkey) d) Military alliance of USSR and her allies. e) Caribbean Islands of Trinidad, Jamaica etc. f) States round the Arabian/Persian Gulf. g) US and USSR normally h) Underdeveloped countries of Africa, Asia and S. America **5** a) US b) Australia c) Japan d) Ireland **6** a) Pakistani/a Pakistani b) Peruvian/a Peruvian c) Thai/a Thai d) Scottish, Scots/a Scotsman, Scotswoman, Scot e) Turkish/a Turk f) Philippine/a Filipino g) Swedish/a Swede h) New Zealand/a New Zealander i) Lebanese/a Lebanese j) Danish/a Dane k) Dutch/a Dutchman, Dutchwoman l) English/an Englishman, Englishwoman m) Iraqi/an Iraqi n) Spanish/a Spaniard o) Finnish/a Finn p) Belgian/a Belgian q) Irish/an Irishman, Irishwoman r) Bangladeshi/a Bangladeshi s) Portuguese/a Portuguese t) French/a Frenchman, Frenchwoman u) Greek/a Greek **7** a) Paris

b) Chicago c) Venice d) Manchester e) Naples
f) Aberdeen g) Milan h) Glasgow i) Liverpool j) Vienna
k) Moscow l) Rome

Names and Titles (p.100)
1 a) surname b) Christian name c) nickname d) alias e) pen-name f) hyphenated name g) maiden name h) pet name i) stage name **2** a) Adm. V.E. Nott R.N. (ret) b) W.P.C. Lockwood c) G.L. Cousins M.A. d) Ms Louise Manners e) Rev. Graham Lee f) Sir Robin Sawyer g) Mrs P. Tucker M.P. h) W.G. Smithson Esq. i) H.R.H. The Prince of Wales j) Jones Bros. k) Z. Wilkins R.A. l) John Fox O.B.E. **3** a) Richard b) Edward c) William d) Albert e) Andrew f) Antony g) Thomas h) Robert i) Elizabeth j) Patricia k) Jennifer l) Margaret m) Jim, Jimmy n) Gerry o) Mike p) Chris q) Joe r) Harry s) Les t) Fred, Freddy u) Pam v) Cath, Cathy w) Sue, Susie x) Di

Foreign Words and Phrases (p.101)
1 a) cul-de-sac b) hors d'oeuvre c) carte blanche d) grand prix e) Bon voyage f) chic g) tête-à-tête h) blasé i) rendezvous j) nouveaux riches **2** a) gourmet b) coup c) entourage d) encore e) C'est la vie f) bloc g) avant garde h) début i) façade j) détente **3** a) bona fide b) curriculum vitae c) pro rata d) persona non grata e) ego f) status quo g) vice versa h) post mortem i) per capita j) ad nauseam **4** a) macho b) kindergarten c) siesta d) graffiti e) kaput f) Bravo g) incognito h) blitz i) kowtow j) patio

Homophones (p.103)
1 a) too b) I c) guessed d) waist e) mail f) weigh g) where h) wore i) hear j) pear k) weight l) steal m) board n) sees, seas o) principle p) court q) whole r) sail s) meat t) passed u) blew v) read w) stares x) borne **2** a) rode, rowed b) sew, sow c) reign, rein d) suite e) fare f) bowled g) minor h) dyed i) sought j) paws k) mane l) pail m) bury n) hire o) threw p) mourning q) prays r) sealing s) herd t) scent, cent u) cell v) coarse w) tyre x) idol

Abbreviations (p.104)
1 a) a.m. (ante meridiem), p.m. (post meridiem) b) PC (Police Constable), CID (Criminal Investigation Department) c) Oxon. (Oxoniensis: of Oxford University), Cantab. (Cantabrigiensis: of Cambridge University) d) MP (Member of Parliament), PM (Prime Minister) e) BR (British Rail), BA (British Airways) f) RN (Royal Navy), RAF (Royal Air Force) g) GMT (Greenwich Mean Time), BST (British Summer Time) h) BBC (British Broadcasting Corporation), IBA (Independent Broadcasting Authority) i) AD (Anno Domini: in the year of Our Lord), BC (Before Christ) **2** a) NHS (National Health Service), GP (General Practitioner), WHO (World Health Organization) b) oz (ounce), lb (pound), st (stone) c) in (inch), ft (foot), yd (yard) d) Con. (Conservative Party), Lab. (Labour Party), SLD (Social and Liberal Democrats) e) St (Street), Rd(Road), Ave (Avenue) f) BA (Bachelor of Arts), MA (Master of Arts), PhD (Doctor of Philosophy) g) mpg (miles per gallon), mph (miles per hour), cc (cubic centimetres) **3** a) HQ (Headquarters) b) DIY (Do It Yourself) c) QC (Queen's Counsel) d) IQ (Intelligence Quotient) e) VC (Victoria Cross) f) TUC (Trades Union Congress) g) PLO (Palestine Liberation Organization) h) VIP (Very Important Person) i) MBE (Member of the British Empire) j) SOS (International distress signal) k) UFO (Unidentified Flying Object) l) CND (Campaign for Nuclear Disarmament) **4** a) VAT (Value Added Tax) b) AIDS (Acquired Immune Deficiency Syndrome) c) NASA (National Aeronautics and Space Administration) d) OPEC (Organization of Petroleum Exporting Countries) e) NATO (North Atlantic Treaty Organization) f) UNESCO (United Nations Educational, Scientific and Cultural Organization)

Similes (p.105)
1 a) hills b) new pin c) dust d) sheet e) feather f) flash g) sandboy h) knife **2** a) drunk b) sober c) poor d) cool e) good f) thin g) fit h) deaf

Proverbs (p.106)
1 a) 4, b) 3, c) 6, d) 1, e) 7, f) 5, g) 8, h) 2 **2** a) 5, b) 2, c) 4, d) 8, e) 7, f) 1, g) 6, h) 3

Euphemisms (p.107)
(other versions possible) **1** a) died b) toilet c) old age pensioners d) dead e) go to the toilet f) was very shabby g) killed.   a) overweight and rather unattractive b) be sick c) is not the best cook in the world d) rather merry e) could have been more carefully done f) is a little slow on his feet **2** a) dismiss Miss Farr b) spying c) poor people d) is in bad condition e) fail f) dangerous g) has been lazy.   a) was not entirely accurate in what he said b) not very fruitful c) has not a very good record of punctuality d) not of the highest quality e) are not as harmonious as they were f) unwise, take industrial action e) we look forward to prompt settlement of your account h) rather displeased

Britain (p.108)
The election system a) General Election b) call an election c) constituencies d) polling day e) campaigns f) canvassing g) polling stations h) secret ballot i) stand for election j) deposit k) eligible l) turn-out m) Member of Parliament n) House of Commons o) by-election p) constituents q) proportional representation **The House of Commons 1** a) benches b) Speaker c) debates d) Opposition e) backbenchers f) Prime Minister g) front bench h) ministers i) Cabinet j) Foreign Secretary k) Home Secretary l) Budget m) Chancellor of the Exchequer n) Leader of the Opposition o) Shadow Cabinet **2** a) Government b) Opposition c) Speaker d) Prime Minister e) Cabinet f) Leader of the Opposition g) Shadow Cabinet h) backbenchers **Famous Places** a) the Old Bailey (Central Criminal Court) b) 10 Downing Street (official residence of Prime Minister) c) Westminster (district where Houses of Parliament are situated) d) Buckingham Palace (residence of the Queen) e) Scotland Yard (police headquarters) f) the City (financial and banking district) g) the West End (entertainment district of big cinemas and theatres) h) Fleet Street (home of many national daily newspapers) i) Whitehall (street where many government ministries are situated) **Places, people, institutions** a) all counties except Manchester, which is a city b) all rivers except Windsor, which is a town c) all islands except Ulster, which is another name for Northern Ireland d) all Prime Ministers except Queen Victoria e) all military or naval heroes except Wren, who was an architect f) all writers except Turner, who was a painter g) all London districts except Brighton, which is a south-coast town h) all London streets except the Cenotaph, which is the national war memorial i) all sporting venues (football, athletics, cricket, tennis) except Heathrow, which is London's main airport j) all political parties except Yellow k) all chain-stores except Harrods, which is a department store l) all capitals (of Scotland, N.Ireland, Wales, England) except Birmingham m) all companies except The British Council, which is a government cultural organization n) all national daily newspapers except Time, which is an American news magazine o) all types of schools except gymnasium, which is a sports and exercise hall p) all banks except the National Trust, which is an organization to protect countryside and historic buildings, monuments q) all London main-line stations except Hampton Court, which is old palace near London r) all prisons except Chequers, which is official country residence of Prime

Minister s) all royal residences except Kew Gardens. which is botanical gardens on the edge of London t) all public schools except Oxford, which is a university u) all sporting events (steeplechase. cricket. football. rowing) except Boxing Day. which is 26 December.